Sensational Party Cakes

Fun and Fancy Cake Decorating Ideas

Romana Gardani

First published in the UK in 2010 by
Apple Press
7 Greenland Street
London NW1 0ND
www.apple-press.com

Published originally under the title
"TORTE CREATIVE" (ISBN 978 88 6154 182 5)
© 2008 Food Editore, an imprint of Food srl,
Parma (www.gruppofood.com)
Via Mazzini, 6 43121 PARMA

Davide Di Prato (photography)
Monia Petrolini (design)

Acknowledgements
Piero Rainone, Licia Cagnoni and Simone Rugiati
for the recipes in the Basic Techniques section
Camilla Cozzini for making the panda shown
on page 89
Antonella Uccelli

ISBN 978 1 84543 392 5

English translation by Sara Harris and Anna
Bennett
© Apple Press

NOTES
Butter: where butter is stipulated, unsalted butter
is meant.
Chocolate: where plain chocolate is stipulated,
70% cocoa solids chocolate is meant.

Printed in China

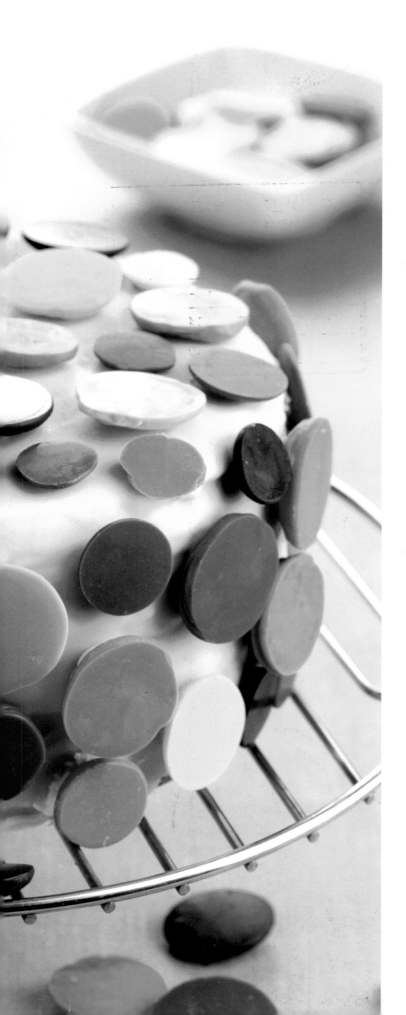

contents

introduction

ONCE UPON A TIME THERE WAS A VICTORIA SPONGE SANDWICH...

Tired of the same old round or square cakes?

Making out-of-the-ordinary cakes that are creative and fun isn't so difficult: start with an idea and be inspired, plan your project and follow a few basic guidelines, and you'll achieve amazing results.

In this book we give suggestions for all sorts of occasions from birthdays to St Valentine's Day and for traditional celebrations, as well as ideas to delight friends who love fashion or gardening, or to celebrate a teenager passing a driving test, the grandparents' wedding anniversary, or just getting good marks at school.

All you need is a little imagination, a good deal of manual dexterity and a handful of sweets and sprinkles to turn your cakes into delightful centrepieces.

Our suggestions do not call for any exceptional cookery skills: we start off with recipes specially chosen for their simplicity, which lend themselves to being transformed into entrancing cakes with irresistible icings and fillings.

This book provides the basics to set you on your way and will enable you to develop a creativity you never knew you possessed. Enjoy the challenge!

basic techniques

basic cake recipes

The cakes and other sweet confections in this section lend themselves particularly well to being filled and covered with sugar paste, almond paste (marzipan), sugar icing or chocolate. Their rich, firm consistency means they are easy to decorate.

sponge cake

ingredients for 4 people 1 x 22-cm cake

4 eggs
150 g caster sugar
150 g plain flour
2 tsp baking powder

❶ Whisk the eggs and sugar over a pan of hot water until pale and frothy.

❷ Remove from the heat and whisk until cool. Fold in the sifted flour and baking powder with a mixing spatula.

❸ Lightly grease a 22-cm spring-release cake tin with butter and dust with flour.

❹ Transfer the cake mixture to the tin and bake in a preheated oven at 180°C/ gas mark 4 for about 30 minutes or until the cake is well risen and golden brown.

Tip
For a lighter sponge cake use icing sugar, halve the quantity of flour and add 75 g cornflour. For a chocolate sponge, add 30 g cocoa powder, sifted with the flour(s)

mocha cake

ingredients for 4 people 1 x 22-cm cake

120 g butter, softened
115 g caster sugar, 2 eggs, 100 g plain flour
3 tbsp cocoa powder, pinch of salt
2 tbsp milk, 1 tsp baking powder
225 ml strong black coffee

❶ Place the butter in the food processor with 100 g of the sugar and mix on low speed until pale and fluffy. Add the lightly beaten eggs, the flour, 2 level tablespoons cocoa powder and a pinch of salt. Process briefly, add 2 tablespoons milk and, lastly, the baking powder. Process very briefly.

❷ Grease a 22-cm soufflé dish and transfer the mixture to it, then mix the remaining cocoa powder and sugar together and sprinkle evenly over the surface. Pour the cold coffee all over the cake and immediately place in a preheated oven at 180°C/gas mark 4 to bake for 30–35 minutes.

buckwheat cake

ingredients for 8 people 1 x 28-cm cake

300 g butter, softened
300g caster sugar
6 eggs, separated
1 tsp vanilla essence, 300 g buckwheat flour
3 tbsp plain flour, 2 tsp baking powder

for the filling
red- or blackcurrant jelly or blueberry jam

❶ Cream the butter and sugar until pale and fluffy; beat in the egg yolks one at a time with a wooden spoon then add the vanilla essence. Sift in both types of flour with the baking powder and stir in gently but thoroughly.

❷ Whisk the egg whites quickly until stiff and fold into the cake mixture immediately. Lightly grease a 28-cm cake tin, dust with flour, and transfer the mixture to it. Bake in a preheated oven at 180°C/ gas mark 4 for at least 45 minutes.

❸ Cut the cake horizontally in half when cold and fill with jelly or blueberry jam.

Tip
When making cakes that are to be filled, try using a tin 4 cm less in diameter than usual. Allow 5–10 minutes more cooking time. The thicker the cake, the easier it is to cut.

orange and lemon drizzle cake

ingredients for 6 people 1 x 26-cm cake

250 g butter, softened
250 g caster sugar
1 unwaxed orange
1 unwaxed lemon
4 eggs
250 g plain flour
1 tsp baking powder
4 tbsp hot water

for the citrus syrup
juice of the orange
juice of the lemon
100 g caster sugar

❶ Cream the butter and sugar until pale and fluffy. Add the finely grated orange and lemon peel. Beat in the eggs one at a time, adding 1–2 tablespoons of the flour as you beat to help the mixture swell in volume. Sift in the remaining flour with the baking powder and stir gently but thoroughly, adding the water last of all. Transfer to a greased 26-cm cake tin lined with greaseproof paper and bake in a preheated oven at 175°C/gas mark 4 for about 30 minutes.

❷ To make the citrus syrup, heat the juice and sugar in a small saucepan over a low heat until the sugar has completely dissolved; boil for 2–3 minutes, uncovered. Remove from the heat and cover to keep warm.

❸ As soon as you remove the cake from the oven, prick numerous holes in it with a cocktail stick and brush the surface with half the syrup. Allow the syrup to soak in for a few minutes, then turn the cake out carefully, upside down, on to a rack and repeat the process with the remaining syrup.

chocolate and aniseed cake

ingredients for 8 people 1 x 24-cm cake

150 g butter, softened
150 g caster sugar
grated peel of ½ unwaxed lemon
3 eggs
300 g plain flour, sifted with 3 tsp baking powder
200 ml milk, 2–3 tbsp Anisette liqueur
2 tbsp cocoa powder, sifted

❶ Grease a 24-cm cake tin with 20 g of the butter.

❷ Beat 130 g butter with the sugar and lemon peel until pale and fluffy. Beat in the eggs one by one. Gradually add the flour and baking powder, alternating with the milk and liqueur, stirring well.

❸ Mix one third of the mixture with the cocoa. Spoon a layer of half the pale mixture into the cake tin; cover with the dark mixture and top with pale mixture. Bake in a preheated oven at 180° C/ gas mark 4 for 45–50 minutes, until well-browned.

Tip
Make sure your cake is cooked by inserting a skewer in the centre: it should come out clean with no trace of cake mixture.

chocolate and ricotta layer cake

ingredients for 6 people 1 x 24-cm cake

150 g plain chocolate
150 g butter, softened
150 g unrefined cane sugar
pinch of salt
6 eggs, separated
150 g plain flour, sifted

for the filling
50 g plain chocolate
200 g very fresh ricotta cheese
70 g chocolate and hazelnut spread
80 ml double cream, whipped

❶ First make the sponge cake: melt the chocolate over a pan of hot water. Cream the butter and sugar with a pinch of salt until pale and fluffy. Stir in the melted chocolate, followed by the egg yolks, one at a time. Whisk the egg whites until stiff and fold into the cake mixture with a mixing spatula, alternating with additions of sifted flour.

❷ Line a 24-cm spring-release cake tin with greaseproof paper, turn the mixture into it and bake in a preheated oven at 160°/gas mark 3 for 50 minutes. Make the filling: melt the chocolate, push the ricotta through a sieve into a bowl and combine with the chocolate and hazelnut spread, followed by the melted chocolate and the whipped cream.

❸ Leave the cake to cool then turn out. Cut horizontally into four layers and add the filling.

walnut cake

ingredients for 6 people 1 x 26-cm cake

185 g butter, softened
95 g unrefined cane sugar, 2 eggs
185 g plain flour, 1 tsp baking powder
pinch of salt, 6 tbsp milk
100 g walnut pieces, chopped

❶ Cream the butter and sugar in a mixing bowl at high speed with a hand-held electric whisk. Lightly beat the eggs then stir into the bowl. Sift in the flour, baking powder and a pinch of salt. Stirring continuously, add the milk a little at a time, followed by 60 g chopped walnuts.

❷ Grease a 26-cm cake tin and dust with flour. Transfer the mixture to it and bake in a preheated oven at 180°/gas mark 4 for 35 minutes. When cooked, allow to cool slightly before turning out.

❸ When cold, cover with chocolate coating (see page 24, substituting 25 g butter for the rum) and sprinkle with 40 g walnuts.

Tip
For an even tastier cake, add 100 g ground hazelnuts or almond paste to the mixture.

lemon cake

ingredients for 6 people 1 x 24-cm cake

250 g butter, softened
250 g caster sugar
4 large eggs (250 g total weight)
125 g plain flour
peel of 1 unwaxed lemon, grated
125 g cornflour
1 tsp baking powder, 1 tbsp milk

❶ Cream the butter with the sugar until pale and fluffy, and stir in the eggs one at a time, adding 1–2 tablespoons of the flour if the mixture does not blend evenly. Add the grated lemon peel.

❷ Sift the flours and baking powder together into the mixture, stirring continuously, and lastly, add the milk.

❸ Grease a 24-cm cake tin, line with greaseproof paper and bake in a preheated oven at 180°C/gas mark 4 for about 1 hour.

yoghurt cake

ingredients for 4 people 1 x 24-cm cake

4 eggs, separated; 170 g caster sugar
pinch of salt, 50 g butter, softened
100 g yoghurt (plain or fruit), 100 g plain flour
100 g cornflour, 2 tsp baking powder
2 tbsp cocoa powder (optional)
30 g icing sugar, sifted

❶ Beat the egg yolks with the sugar and salt until pale. Stir in the butter and yoghurt. Sift the flours and baking powder together into the bowl, stirring continuously. If using the cocoa powder, add it to the bowl with the flours.

❷ Whisk the egg whites until stiff, then whisk in the icing sugar and fold into the cake mixture. For a quicker, less airy cake, place all the ingredients in the food processor and mix until smooth.

❸ Grease a 24-cm cake tin and transfer the mixture to it. Bake in a preheated oven at 170°C/gas mark 3 for about 30 minutes.

carrot cake

ingredients for 8 people 1 x 26-cm cake

200 g butter, softened
150 g caster sugar
8 egg yolks plus 6 egg whites
260 g plain flour
2 tsp baking powder
350 g finely grated carrots, blotted dry
110 g ground almonds
60 ml double cream
75 g icing sugar, sifted

❶ Cream the butter with the caster sugar until pale and fluffy and stir in the egg yolks one at a time.

❷ Sift in the flour with the baking powder while stirring, followed by the carrots, almonds and cream.

❸ Whisk the egg whites until stiff, then whisk in the icing sugar. Fold into the cake mixture. Grease a 26-cm cake tin and line with greaseproof paper. Bake in a preheated oven at 185°C/gas mark 4 for about 50 minutes.

Tip
You can also use a rectangular or square tin for this cake.

12

milk chocolate and citrus cake

ingredients for 4 people 1 x 20-cm cake

150 g milk chocolate, in small pieces
½ tbsp grated unwaxed lemon peel
½ tbsp grated unwaxed orange peel
60 g plain flour
95 g blanched almonds
4 eggs
125 g caster sugar
2 tbsp warm milk
pinch of salt
½ tsp baking powder
170 ml double cream

❶ Grease a 20-cm spring-release cake tin and line the bottom with greaseproof paper. Place 100 g of the chocolate with the grated lemon and orange peel in a food processor, and process briefly until the chocolate is finely chopped. Add the flour and almonds and process briefly again. Beat the egg yolks and sugar in a bowl with a hand-held electric whisk until pale, and fold in the contents of the food processor and the milk.

❷ Whisk the egg whites with a pinch of salt until stiff and gently fold in the chocolate cake mixture, using a mixing spatula, followed by the baking powder. Transfer to the prepared cake tin. Bake in a preheated oven at 180°C/gas mark 4 for 45 minutes. When cooked, turn out immediately on to a rack to allow excess moisture to evaporate. Chill in the refrigerator for 30 minutes before cutting horizontally in half.

❸ Melt the remaining chocolate over a pan of hot water and spread over the lower layer of the cake. Top this with whipped cream and cover with the upper cake layer. Chill in the refrigerator for 20 minutes.

chocolate and Amaretto cake

ingredients for 6 people 1 x 22-cm cake

300 g blanched almonds
200 g caster sugar, 5 eggs
280 g plain chocolate, coarsely chopped
100 g butter, 2–3 tbsp Amaretto liqueur
1 tsp almond essence (optional)
½ tsp vanilla essence, 3 tbsp cornflour
pinch of salt, 2 tsp baking powder

❶ Grind the almonds (not too finely) with the sugar in a food processor and transfer to a mixing bowl. Using a balloon whisk, beat in the eggs vigorously, one at a time. Melt the chocolate with the butter over hot water, remove from the hob and keep warm. Stir the Amaretto, vanilla, almond essence if used, cornflour and a pinch of salt into the mixing bowl.

❷ Add the melted chocolate and butter mixture followed by the baking powder, stirring until smooth. Grease a 22-cm spring-release cake tin, dust with flour and line with greaseproof paper. Bake in a preheated oven at 180°C/gas mark 4 for 45 minutes.

Tip
Do not process the almonds and sugar for too long or the nuts will heat up and release their plentiful almond oil content.

Sachertorte

ingredients for 4 people 2 x 22-cm cakes

200 g plain chocolate, in small pieces
8 egg yolks plus 10 egg whites
125 g butter, at room temperature
1 tsp vanilla essence, 150 g icing sugar, sifted
pinch of salt, 120 g plain flour
½ tsp baking powder

for the filling and glaze
200 g apricot jam, melted and sieved

for the icing
90 g plain chocolate, 200 ml double cream
150 g icing sugar, sifted; 1 egg yolk,

❶ Melt the chocolate in a bowl over a pan of hot water. Allow to cool slightly. Beat the egg yolks lightly in a mixing bowl and stir in the melted chocolate. Stir in 100 g very soft butter, the vanilla essence and the sugar.

❷ Whisk the 10 egg whites with a pinch of salt until stiff and fold one third of them into the chocolate mixture, using a mixing spatula. Fold in the flour, followed by the remaining beaten egg whites and the baking powder.

❸ Grease 2 x 22-cm cake tins and dust with flour. Transfer half the mixture into each tin. Bake in a preheated oven at 170°/gas mark 3 for 35 minutes. Turn out and leave to cool then spread some of the warm, sieved apricot jam between the two layers, sandwich together and use the rest of the jam to glaze the cake.

❹ Make the icing: melt the chocolate with the cream and sugar in a bowl over barely simmering water, stirring with a mixing spatula. Cook for 5 minutes without stirring. Beat the egg yolk in a cup, mix in 3 tablespoons of the chocolate mixture and pour back into the bowl, stirring continuously. After 1 minute, pour the thick chocolate coating all over the glazed cake. Chill for at least 3 hours before serving.

chocolate and almond cake

ingredients for 6 people 1 x 26-cm cake

300 g plain chocolate, in small pieces
250 g butter
5 eggs
4 tbsp caster sugar
100 g ground almonds
150 g plain flour, sifted
2 tsp baking powder

❶ Melt the chocolate with the butter in a bowl over gently simmering water, stirring until smooth. Remove from the heat. Beat the eggs with the sugar until pale and foamy and stir in the ground almonds, the flour and baking powder, followed by the melted chocolate mixture.

❷ Lightly grease a 26-cm spring-release cake tin and dust with flour, transfer the mixture to it and bake in a preheated oven at 160°C/gas mark 3 for 45 minutes. Allow the cake to cool completely in the tin before turning it out.

14

cinnamon and orange cake

ingredients for 6 people 1 x 26-cm cake

200 g butter, softened
200 g caster sugar
1 tbsp finely chopped orange peel
    (fresh or candied)
4 eggs, separated
200 g plain flour
2 tsp baking powder
1 tsp cinnamon
pinch of salt
200 g ground almonds

❶ Cream the butter vigorously with the sugar until pale then stir in the orange peel and the egg yolks, one at a time. Sift the flour with the baking powder and cinnamon. Whisk the egg whites with a pinch of salt in a large bowl until stiff, and gently but thoroughly fold in alternating small amounts of ground almonds, the flour, baking powder and cinnamon mixture, and the egg yolk and butter mixture.

❷ Grease a 26-cm cake tin, line with greaseproof paper and transfer the mixture to it. Bake in a preheated oven at 170°C/gas mark 3 for about 50 minutes.

Tip
Never heat butter to soften it. Cut into small pieces, leave in a warm kitchen and then cream it if necessary.

cupcakes

ingredients for 6 cupcakes

60 g butter
250 g plain flour
125 g caster sugar or 125 g icing
   sugar, sifted
1 egg, lightly beaten
250 ml milk
pinch of salt
2 tsp baking powder

❶ Melt the butter in a bowl over a pan of hot water. Sift the flour and sugar into a mixing bowl and stir in the egg, melted butter, milk, salt and baking powder. Mix until smooth.

❷ Spoon the mixture into paper cases or a non-stick cupcake baking tray, filling each only two thirds full.

❸ Bake in a preheated oven at 175°C/ gas mark 4 for 20–25 minutes, until golden brown on top.

chocolate cupcakes

ingredients for 10 cupcakes

200 g hazelnuts, toasted and skinned
180 g butter
6 egg whites
155 g plain flour
250 g icing sugar
30 g cocoa powder

❶ Finely grind the hazelnuts in a food processor. Heat the butter in a small saucepan for 4 minutes, until it colours slightly. Leave to cool.

❷ Whisk the egg whites until stiff. Sift the flour, sugar and cocoa powder into a mixing bowl, add the ground hazelnuts and fold in the egg whites and the melted butter gently but thoroughly.

❸ Spoon the mixture into paper cases or a non-stick cupcake baking tray, filling each only half full. Bake at 200°C/gas mark 6 for 20–25 minutes then insert a cocktail stick to check they are cooked in the centre. Leave to cool.

meringues

ingredients for 12 meringues

100 g egg whites
200 g caster sugar

❶ Place the egg whites in a large mixing bowl, making sure there are no traces of yolk. Add the sugar and whisk.

❷ Continue whisking until stiff peaks form when the beaters are lifted out of the meringue mixture.

❸ Cover 1 or more baking sheets with greaseproof paper and use a piping bag and fluted nozzle to pipe out 12 meringues. Meringues are best cooked at an extremely low temperature, taking 1–3 hours, depending on size, gradually drying and hardening, but they can be cooked more quickly, at 100°C/about gas mark ¼.

You can use food colouring for your meringues, adding this when whisking the egg whites stiffly.

Tip
For really successful meringues, turn off the oven when they are cooked and leave them there to cool completely.

biscuit mixture

ingredients for 20–30 small biscuits

140 g butter, softened
360 g plain flour, 120 g cornflour, 200 g caster sugar
grated peel of 1 unwaxed lemon (optional)
pinch of salt, 2 eggs

❶ Mix together the butter, flours, sugar, grated lemon peel if used and salt either by rubbing in or with a pastry blender. Add the eggs and work briefly, preferably by hand, until blended and smooth. Chill in the refrigerator for 30 minutes.

❷ Roll the mixture out on to greaseproof paper and cut out shapes using pastry cutters. Bake on baking sheets in a preheated oven at 180°/gas mark 4 for 15–20 minutes, depending on how well-browned you like them.

fillings for cakes

Your cakes will be even more irresistible if you fill them with soft, creamy mixtures, especially when your cake design calls for very thick cakes which would otherwise tend to be dry.

chocolate cream

ingredients to fill 1 x 30-cm cake

500 ml double cream, 250 g chocolate and hazelnut spread

Whip the cream and gently fold in the chocolate and hazelnut spread with a mixing spatula.

lemon filling

ingredients to fill 1 x 24-cm cake

30 g cornflour, 100 g caster sugar, 150 ml cold water 25 g butter, 1 egg, 2 unwaxed lemons

Mix the cornflour and sugar in a small saucepan with a wooden spoon, gradually adding the water. Place on a gentle heat, add the butter and bring up to the boil, stirring continuously.

As soon as the mixture has thickened, remove from the heat and lightly beat the egg and stir into the mixture, followed by the grated lemon peel of 1 lemon and juice of both lemons. Cover with clingfilm and leave to cool.

chocolate and hazelnut confectioner's custard

ingredients to fill 1 x 22-cm cake

50 g plain chocolate, coarsely grated 500 g confectioner's custard 400 g chocolate and hazelnut spread

Add the chocolate to the warm confectioner's custard as soon as you remove it from the heat and stir until melted. Leave to cool before gently stirring in the spread.

confectioner's custard

ingredients to fill 1 x 30–32 cm cake

1 litre milk, 1 vanilla pod 200 g caster sugar 6 egg yolks 120 g plain flour icing sugar, sifted

Heat the milk slowly to boiling point with the vanilla pod in it. Whisk the sugar and egg yolks in a bowl until pale, add the sifted flour and stir until smooth. Gradually add the hot milk, whisking continuously. Return to the milk saucepan and cook gently, stirring continuously, until the custard has thickened. Remove from the heat when it begins to boil, and take out the vanilla pod and discard. Pour the custard into a bowl, sprinkle the surface with a little icing sugar and place clingfilm on top, ensuring that this makes contact with the custard's surface (this prevents a skin from forming). Refrigerate until needed.

coffee confectioner's cream

Before cooking the custard mixture (above), add 2–3 tablespoons strong black coffee. The same quantity of strong coffee can also be added to the chocolate cream recipe, top left.

coverings

These sweet pastes for cake coverings are malleable and easy to use, forming a perfectly smooth covering, ready for decorating with your most original and imaginative designs.

sugar paste

for 1 x 28-cm cake

500 g icing sugar
1 egg white
30 ml glucose syrup

Sift the icing sugar into a mixing bowl and stir in the other ingredients; work until you have a smooth, firm, homogenous mixture; and add a few drops of water if the paste is too hard. You can use a food processor to make sugar paste. Wrap the paste tightly in clingfilm and store in a sealed plastic container. It will retain its elasticity for about 1 month.

marshmallow sugar paste

for 1 x 22-cm cake

200 g marshmallows
4 tbsp water
200g icing sugar, sifted

Heat the marshmallows with the water in a bowl over gently simmering water until melted. Remove from the heat and stir in most of the icing sugar. Sprinkle a work surface with icing sugar and place the thick paste on it. Work the paste by hand, adding more sifted icing sugar if needed. Wrap tightly in clingfilm and leave at room temperature for 24 hours before using.

almond paste (marzipan)

for 1 x 22-cm cake

220g ground almonds
220 g icing sugar, sifted plus 30 g for the work surface
1 tsp lemon juice
1 tsp almond essence
2 egg whites

Combine all the ingredients and work together by hand (or you can use a food processor) until the almond paste is smooth and homogenous enough to roll out. If it is too hard, add a little more egg white; if too soft, work in more icing sugar. Always sprinkle the work surface and the rolling pin with icing sugar when rolling out the paste. Wrap tightly in clingfilm; it will keep for up to 1 month in the refrigerator.

Tip
You can buy ready-made slabs of almond paste (marzipan) and sugar paste. Sugar paste can be rolled out more thinly than almond paste, which tends to break up more easily.

preparing the cake for covering

To ensure the sugar paste or almond paste sticks to the cake, you must first glaze the cake's surface with a thin layer of melted, sieved apricot jam.

rolling out sugar or almond paste

Knead the paste to soften it and sprinkle the work surface and rolling pin with icing sugar before rolling out.

completing the covering

Gently press the paste against the cake, using your hands, to make it stick all over then cut off excess paste with a pastry cutter or a sharp knife. Use the trimmings for your decorations.

placing the covering over the cake

Sprinkle the surface of the paste and the rolling pin with icing sugar, roll the paste up around the rolling pin, then carefully unroll it to cover the cake.

sugar paste and almond paste creations

modelling

Knead the sugar paste or almond paste to soften before working it into your chosen shapes. Stick small parts on with a damp paintbrush but secure larger pieces with a cocktail stick.

colouring

Dip a cocktail stick in some water-soluble colouring and transfer a few drops to the sugar paste or almond paste. The colouring is very concentrated; add a very little at a time and knead the paste until it is evenly coloured throughout. For pale colours you will need very little colouring; it will take only a tiny quantity of red to produce pink, or of basic blue for light blue.

To give a shiny finish to sugar paste or almond paste coverings, brush the surface with a thin film of melted, sieved apricot jam mixed with a very little water. Use sparingly or you will dissolve the sugar.

joining small cakes

Use cocktail sticks to join cupcakes to form special shapes, adapting the joins as necessary (see various recipes). Make sure you join them before the icing has set and hardened.

tiered cakes: reinforcing the base

To support upper layers, strengthen the cake base with wooden skewers, trimmed to lengths equal to the lower layer's height, pushed into it until they are barely visible.

building tiered cakes

Spread a little fresh, unset icing between the reinforcing sticks of the bottom layer. Put the upper layer on a cardboard disc and place it on top. This method can be used for up to three layers if the cakes are not too heavy, otherwise you will need plastic cake supports available from specialised cake-decorating suppliers.

cutting out shapes

Cut out the pattern in thin card, place it on the cake (before applying the warm apricot glaze) and hold firmly in place; use a serrated knife, held vertically, to cut all around the outline for a neat shape.

icing

Soft when you spread it, icing hardens as it sets. You can completely cover large cakes and cupcakes or choose to adorn them with even easier piped-icing decorations.

royal icing

ingredients for 1 x 20-cm cake

200 g icing sugar, sifted
1 egg white
few drops of lemon juice

Combine the egg white and a few drops of lemon juice with the icing sugar in a bowl. Mix very thoroughly. The icing should be fairly fluid (see page 23, liquid icing).

This icing keeps well in an airtight container for 7 days but, if not used within 24 hours, it will separate and must be stirred again until smooth.

colouring icing

Buy water-soluble gel or liquid food colourings. Dip the tip of a cocktail stick into the colouring and then dip it into the icing. Mix vigorously until evenly coloured. Add a little more colouring at a time to reach the shade you require.

Tip
Always sift icing sugar before using it to prevent lumps from forming. Depending on the decorating task and the consistency required, use more or less icing sugar. If you cannot buy disposable piping bags, you can make your own with a triangle of greaseproof paper.

22

Sensational Party Cakes

thick icing

Icing for piping decorations or writing must be fairly thick: lift the spoon from the mixture, which should be stiff enough to retain its shape, with peaks that stay upright. Add more icing sugar if necessary to thicken. Piping bags and nozzles are always used with this consistency, to cover or decorate cakes as shown in these photographs.

liquid icing

Coating or liquid icing should be of 'ribbon' consistency: when you allow some mixture to fall from a spoon held above the bowl, it should fall in a 'ribbon' that does not break for about 2 seconds.

coating with icing Liquid icing is used to coat cakes: pour it directly from the bowl over the cake; it will spread of its own accord, or with the help of a spatula or palette knife. Allow to harden before serving. Always glaze a cake with a thin film of warm, sieved apricot jam before coating with icing.

decorating with icing To make small decorative motifs (called 'run outs'), place greaseproof paper on a square of polystyrene and secure with pins, pipe out the outline with thick icing, then fill this outline with liquid icing, using a cocktail stick to fill tight corners.

chocolate coating

ingredients for 1 x 22-cm cake

400 g plain chocolate, in small pieces
25 ml dark rum (optional)

Melt the chocolate in a bowl over hot water, add the rum if used and stir. Pour the chocolate coating over the cake placed on a rack.

butter and cocoa powder cream

ingredients for 1 x 30-cm cake

250 g butter, softened; 500 g icing sugar, sifted
1 tbsp cocoa powder, sifted then mixed with
 1 tbsp hot water

Cream the butter with a wooden spoon until it is pale and fluffy, and gradually beat in the icing sugar, followed by the cocoa powder. Add your choice of extra flavouring if wished.

chocolate ganache

ingredients for 1 x 20-cm cake

200 g plain chocolate, in small pieces
50 g butter, 25 ml double cream

Melt the chocolate and butter together in a bowl over hot water then add the cream and stir until very smooth and hot. Allow to cool before spreading with a palette knife.

24

Tip
For a really shiny finish, soften 8 g leaf gelatine in cold water, blot dry, then add to the chocolate and allow both to melt completely.

Tip
Chocolate coating can also be made with white chocolate.

tempering chocolate

This process results in a glossy, even coating when using chocolate for dipping or moulding. Melt the chocolate, broken into small pieces, in a bowl placed over a pan of very gently simmering water or in the microwave. Keep stirring with a silicone spatula and heating until it reaches 45°C (use a kitchen thermometer). It should be liquid and smooth.

Pour three quarters of the chocolate on to a marble or acrylic slab and spread it out evenly. Work the chocolate: scoop it up and turn it over several times. Leave for a few minutes to cool to 27°C, when it will have partially solidified. Return it to the bowl containing the remaining chocolate and heat to 32°C, stirring gently with the spatula. It should be very glossy. Make sure the chocolate stays melted and use it at once.

decorating with chocolate

The simplest way of decorating with chocolate is just to melt it, put it in a piping bag and pipe designs directly on to the cake, or pipe on to greaseproof paper, leave to harden and transfer to the cake. To make chocolate shapes with plain, milk and white chocolate, melt these in separate bowls over hot water. Divide the white chocolate between as many bowls as you have colours and colour with fat-soluble food colouring. Place greaseproof paper as tracing paper over the required designs and fill several greaseproof paper piping bags with the various melted chocolates. Snip off the tip of the plain chocolate bag and pipe the outlines and any details. Leave briefly to set. Use the other colours to fill in these outlines, allowing the first layer to set before piping a different colour or detail on top of it.

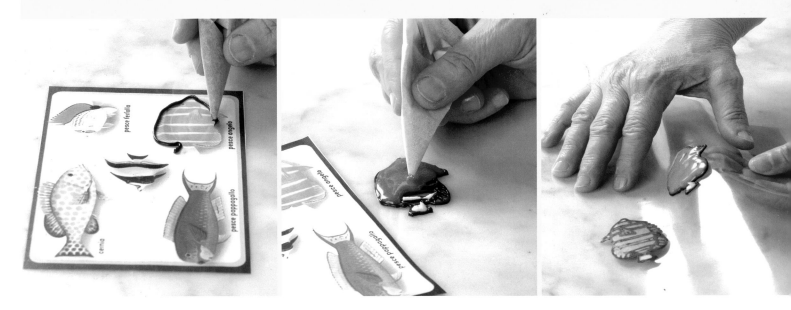

essential equipment

sifter, silicone or aluminium baking moulds, food colourings (water-soluble for sugar or marzipan and fat-soluble for chocolate), paper cupcake cases, cake racks, pastry cutting wheel, ruler, paintbrush, pastry brush, wooden skewers, food marker pen, small spreader knife, flexible spatula nozzles, wafers, cocktail sticks...

...rolling pin, palette knife, ribbons, coloured gels for writing and decoration, pastry cutters, garlic press (or use a ricer, for making hair or grass), piping bags, rotary parsley cutter (for cutting even strips), small roller.

decorating with sugar...

sugared and chocolate-coated almonds, mint pastilles, soft or crunchy sweets, sugar hearts and flowers (stick them on with icing and use them to outline design details), hundreds-and-thousands, Smarties, M&Ms, coloured sugar (sprinkle them over your cakes or use for decorative edgings)...

...multi-coloured jelly sweets, marshmallows, red-and-black liquorice strips, chocolate sticks, strips of special chewing gum (all of these are perfect for trimming to size with scissors or with a small, sharp knife for transformation into all sorts of decorative designs).

...and sweets

polka dot cake 32, tiered cake with red berries 34, handbag cake 36, platform shoe 38, cupcake pyramid 40, fluttering butterflies 42, multi-coloured spangle cake 44, rainbow cake 46, FIAT 500 48, pop-art flower biscuits 50, dice cake 52, Mondrian cake 54, op-art cake 56, sunflower cake 58, prize allotment 60, frosted rosebud cake 62, black-and-white biscuits 63, stamp motif cake 64, three-tier bonbon cake 66

sensational party cakes
for every occasion

polka dot cake

you will need

3 square cakes:
   16 cm, 12 cm and 8 cm
200 g apricot jam
1.5 kg sugar paste
lilac water-soluble gel colouring
icing sugar, sifted
20 g white icing
2 x cardboard squares: 11 cm and 7 cm
pastry brush
rolling pin
pastry cutting wheel
wooden skewers
1.5 m lilac satin ribbon

Place each of the 2 smaller cakes on a cardboard square. Place the largest cake directly on the serving plate. Microwave the apricot jam for 1 minute or heat for 3–4 minutes over hot water (push through a sieve once melted). Using a pastry brush, spread the 3 cakes with a layer of warm jam.

1. Mix about 1.2 kg of the sugar paste thoroughly with lilac gel to colour evenly. Dust the work surface and rolling pin with icing sugar and roll the sugar paste out into a 3–4-mm thick sheet, large enough to cover all three cakes, sides included. Measure and cut out a piece to cover the largest cake.

2. Sprinkle the surface of the paste and the rolling pin with more icing sugar, roll the paste up around the rolling pin, then carefully unroll it to cover the cake completely. Cover the 2 smaller cakes in the same way. Using a pastry cutting wheel or a small sharp knife, cut off any excess paste.

3. Cut 4 pieces of wooden skewer to the height of the bottom layer and push them into the centre in a square pattern (they will support the upper layers). Spread a little white icing between them and place the next cake on top, taking care to centre it accurately. Repeat the process with 4 more pieces of skewer in this middle layer; spread a little white icing between them and place the top layer in the exact centre.

4. Measure and cut the lilac ribbon to size to surround the bottom layer and fix it in place with a little white icing. Do likewise with the next 2 layers. Roll the reserved white sugar paste out and cut out your chosen size of polka dots. Stick them to the cake surface using a pastry brush dampened with water. Place a sugar paste flower on top.

tiered cake
with red berries

Sensational Party Cakes

you will need
2 cakes: 22 cm and 14 cm
200 g apricot jam
1.4 kg white sugar paste
(800 g of which to colour)
pink water-soluble gel colouring
icing sugar, sifted
20 g white icing
assorted red berries,
wild or cultivated
1 x 13-cm cardboard disc
pastry brush
rolling pin
pastry cutting wheel
pinking shears
wooden skewers
pastry brush

Place the smaller cake on the cardboard disc and the larger cake directly on the serving plate. Microwave the apricot jam for 1 minute or heat for 3–4 minutes over hot water (push through a sieve once melted). Using a pastry brush, spread the cakes with a layer of warm jam. Mix 800 g of the sugar paste thoroughly with pink gel to colour evenly. Dust the work surface and rolling pin with icing sugar and roll the sugar paste out into a 3–4·mm thick sheet, large enough to cover both cakes, sides included. Measure and cut out a piece large enough to cover the larger cake. Using a pastry cutting wheel or a small sharp knife, cut off any excess sugar paste. Cover the smaller cake in the same way.

1. Make the 'doilies': roll the reserved white sugar paste out then select 2 cake or flan tins, each larger in diameter than their respective cakes. Press gently on to the paste and use the pinking shears to cut around these circular impressions. Make little dimples near the edges with the tip of a skewer.

2. Dampen the top of the larger cake with a moistened pastry brush and place the sugar paste doily on top.

3. Insert 4 pieces of wooden skewer, trimmed to the height of the lower layer into the cake's centre, arranged in a triangle (to support the upper layer). Spread a little white icing between them and carefully place the smaller cake on top, accurately centred. Dampen the surface of the smaller cake with a moistened pastry brush and cover with its doily. Rinse and thoroughly dry the berries then arrange them around and on top of the cakes.

The perfect gift to delight an ultra-chic friend or to herald a longed-for present of the real thing!

handbag cake

you will need
1 x 18-cm cake
200 g apricot jam
filling of your choice (optional)
400 g sugar paste or
   almond paste
red water-soluble gel colouring
   or a colour of your choice
icing sugar, sifted
red or black liquorice strips, narrow
   and broad
2 gold foil-wrapped sweets
pastry brush
rolling pin
pastry cutting wheel
cocktail sticks

Cut the cake vertically in half to form two semicircles, and place one on top of the other with a layer of apricot jam (or your choice of filling) between them. Cut out the cake to shape, using the template on page 117. Microwave the apricot jam for 1 minute or heat for 3–4 minutes over hot water (push through a sieve once melted). Using a pastry brush, spread the cakes with a layer of warm jam.

1. Mix the sugar paste or almond paste thoroughly with your chosen colouring to colour evenly. Dust the work surface and rolling pin with icing sugar and roll the paste out into a 3–4-mm thick sheet, large enough to cover the entire cake, sides included.

2. Sprinkle the surface of the paste and the rolling pin with more icing sugar, roll the paste up around the rolling pin, then carefully unroll it to cover the cake completely. Using a pastry cutting wheel or a small sharp knife, cut off any excess sugar paste.

3. Cut a suitable length of the broader liquorice strip for the handle and attach to the 'bag'. Insert a cocktail stick halfway into each end and push the exposed half of the cocktail sticks into the cake.

4. Press 2 foil-wrapped sweets into the centre to make the clasp.

5. Cut the thin liquorice strips into 1-cm lengths and press into the paste along the upper and side edges to represent the stitching.

For the fashion-conscious girl who adores very high heels even though they may lead to a fall, and for anyone who's bored with cakes that are no fun at all.

platform shoe

Sensational Party Cakes

you will need
1 x 18-cm cake
chocolate cream
  (see recipe on page 17)
200 g apricot jam
500 g sugar paste (400 g of which
  to colour)
red and brown water-soluble
  gel colouring
icing sugar, sifted
pastry brush
rolling pin
pastry cutting wheel

Cut out a shoe shape on card using the template on page 118, place it on the cake and cut out the shape of the shoe, using a serrated knife held vertically. Cut the cake horizontally in half and fill with plenty of chocolate cream. Place the cake on a serving plate. Microwave the apricot jam for 1 minute or heat for 3–4 minutes over hot water (push through a sieve once melted). Using a pastry brush, spread the cakes with a layer of warm jam.

1. Mix 200 g of the sugar paste with the red gel to make your chosen shade of pink. Dust the work surface and rolling pin with icing sugar. Roll the pink paste out into a 4–5-mm thick sheet, large enough to cover the cake, sides (but not the heel) included. Sprinkle the surface of the paste and the rolling pin with more icing sugar, roll the paste up around the rolling pin, then carefully unroll it to cover the cake completely, except for the heel. Using a pastry cutting wheel or a small sharp knife, cut off any excess sugar paste.

2. Roll 50 g of the white sugar paste out thinly, cut out a semicircle and moisten the shoe's upper front section with a damp pastry brush, then fit the paste over it.

3. Colour most of the remaining sugar paste dark brown, roll it out and cover the heel and platform sole. Colour the last of the paste light brown, then cut out a rectangle and attach to the underside of the shoe, between the sole and the heel.

You can use plain or chocolate cupcakes for this creation and you may choose to add a filling of your favourite jam.

cupcake pyramid

Sensational Party Cakes

you will need
for a pyramid with a 28-cm base:
    35 chocolate cupcakes (see recipe
    on page 15), baked in white,
    green, red, yellow and blue fluted
    paper cases
500 g royal icing
green, red, yellow and blue
    water-soluble gel colouring
piping bag and 3-mm nozzle
spreading knife or palette knife
serving plate or cake stand

Up to 2 days in advance, make little sugar decorations with some of the icing in appropriate colours, using piping bags with a fine nozzle. Pipe out stars, zigzags, flowers, bows, moons etc. on to greaseproof paper; leave these to dry and harden.

Work out your cupcake colour scheme in advance if you bake the cakes in coloured paper cases: the higher the layer, the fewer of each colour if you copy the design shown opposite.

1. Using a spreading knife or palette knife, apply an even covering of white icing to all but 4 cakes. Colour sufficient batches of icing so that 1 cake will match each layer's paper cases (for example, green icing to match green cases).

2. When you have iced all the cupcakes, arrange them on the cake stand, each layer having matching paper cases and one cake iced with the same colour. Press each cake gently into the icing of the cakes below it to make the pyramid stable.

3. Press the prepared decorations very gently on to the icing of the cakes before it sets; if it has hardened, dip a cocktail stick into a little freshly made liquid icing and use as your adhesive.

fluttering butterflies

Sensational Party Cakes

you will need
For the cake
3 cakes: 22 cm, 18 cm and 14 cm
200 g apricot jam
icing sugar, sifted
1.2 kg white sugar paste
pastry brush
rolling pin
pastry cutting wheel
2 x cardboard discs:
   17 cm and 13 cm
wooden skewers

For 10 butterflies
400 g white royal icing
water-soluble gel colourings
   of your choice
rice noodles
greaseproof paper
1 sheet polystyrene
piping bags
foam rubber

Make the butterflies 2–3 days in advance, in 2 stages, starting with the wings. Follow the instructions on page 23, using the template on page 118. Leave the wings to dry for 24 hours before detaching them gently from the greaseproof paper. Make the butterflies' bodies and insert a pair of wings into each body, propping them up in position with pieces of foam. Push pieces of rice noodle into their heads for their antennae and leave to dry.

For the cake: place the largest cake on a serving plate. Microwave the apricot jam for 1 minute or heat for 3–4 minutes over hot water (push through a sieve once melted). Using a pastry brush, spread the cakes with a layer of warm jam. Dust the work surface and rolling pin with icing sugar and roll the sugar paste out into a 4–5-mm thick sheet, large enough to cover all 3 cakes, sides included. Measure and cut out a piece to cover the largest cake. Sprinkle the surface of the paste and the rolling pin with more icing sugar, roll the paste up around the rolling pin, then carefully unroll it to cover the cake completely. Using a pastry cutting wheel or a small sharp knife, cut off any excess sugar paste.

1. Place the 2 smaller cakes on cardboard discs, and glaze and cover in the same way. Reinforce and assemble the cakes as described on page 21.

2. Fill a piping bag fitted with a round nozzle with royal icing and mask the joins with a decorative design.

3. Decorate the cake with the butterflies, sticking the underside of each to its surface with a little royal icing.

This brightly coloured, amusing and scrumptious cake will delight all chocoholics: the decorations are all in various shades of chocolate.

multi-coloured
spangle cake

you will need
2 x 18-cm cakes
200 g apricot jam
500 g white chocolate, for coating
50 g milk chocolate, for
  the spangles
50 g plain chocolate, for
  the spangles
250 g white chocolate, for
  the spangles
red, blue, yellow, orange and
  green fat-soluble food colouring
  for chocolate
pastry brush
1 x 17-cm cardboard disc
greaseproof paper
2 sheets foil

Spread your choice of filling between the 2 cakes then sandwich the cakes together. Microwave the apricot jam for 1 minute or heat for 3–4 minutes over hot water (push through a sieve once melted). Using a pastry brush, spread the cake with a layer of warm jam. Put the cake on the cardboard disc and place on a cake rack over a large plate. Melt 500 g white chocolate in the microwave or over hot water and pour over the cake, coating its top and sides. Leave to set, then transfer to a serving plate.

1. While the cake covering is hardening, prepare the chocolate spangles: make 7 piping bags out of triangles of greaseproof paper, folding them into cone-shaped bags. Melt the milk, plain and 250 g white chocolate in 3 separate bowls over hot water or in the microwave. Fill 2 piping bags with the plain and milk chocolate. Snip the pointed end of each bag before piping blobs of chocolate, spaced apart, on to the sheets of foil.

2. Divide the melted white chocolate between 5 bowls, keeping a little aside. Colour these red, blue, yellow, orange and green. Fill each of the remaining piping bags with a different colour, snip off their tips and pipe more chocolate blobs on to the foil. Chill all the spangles in the refrigerator until they harden and come away from the foil, and use drops of the remaining white chocolate to stick them to the cake.

An elegant cake to prepare for friends who will appreciate its cheerful stripes, allowing you to show off your dexterity and colour sense.

rainbow cake

Sensational Party Cakes

you will need
1 x 16-cm square sponge cake
200 g apricot jam
icing sugar, sifted
700 g sugar paste (300 g of which
   to colour)
yellow, blue, orange, red, pink
   and brown water-soluble
   gel colouring
pastry brush
rolling pin
pastry cutting wheel

Place the cake on a serving plate. Microwave the apricot jam for 1 minute or heat for 3–4 minutes over hot water (push through a sieve once melted). Using a pastry brush, spread the cake with a layer of warm jam. Dust the work surface and rolling pin with icing sugar and roll 400 g of the white sugar paste out into a 3–4-mm thick sheet, large enough to cover the whole cake, sides included. Sprinkle the surface of the paste and the rolling pin with more icing sugar, roll the paste up around the rolling pin, then carefully unroll it to cover the cake completely. Using a pastry cutting wheel or a small sharp knife, cut off any excess sugar paste.

1. Divide the remaining sugar paste into the same number of batches as your chosen colours and colour them.

2. Roll the coloured batches of sugar paste out, one at a time, and cut them into neat strips, some wider than others, long enough to stretch over the cake and down two sides. Dampen the surface of the iced cake slightly with a moistened pastry brush. Working across the cake from the far side, put the strips neatly in place, in varying widths and colours, so that they completely cover the top and two sides. Cover the remaining 2 sides with coloured strips. Trim off any excess sugar paste with a sharp, pointed knife.

FIAT 500

you will need
1 x rectangular cake: 20 x 15 cm
200 g apricot jam
600 g sugar paste
yellow, black and red
  water-soluble gel colouring
icing sugar, sifted
greaseproof paper
pastry brush
rolling pin
pastry cutting wheel
paintbrush

Trace the car's template on page 119 using greaseproof paper or cut out a copy on card. Place the template on the cake and cut round it, using a serrated knife held vertically so as to achieve a neat outline without damaging the cake. Place the cake on a serving plate. Microwave the apricot jam for 1 minute or heat for 3–4 minutes over hot water (push through a sieve once melted). Using a pastry brush, spread the cake with a layer of warm jam.

1. Colour 475 g of the sugar paste yellow, reserving the rest for the various contrasting parts. Dust the work surface and rolling pin with icing sugar and roll the yellow sugar paste out into a 3–4-mm thick sheet, large enough to cover the whole cake and its sides.

2. Sprinkle the surface of the paste and the rolling pin with more icing sugar, roll the paste up around the rolling pin, then carefully unroll it to cover the cake completely.

3. Cut out the windows and bumpers from the reserved white paste and dampen the surface with a moistened pastry brush, then stick them in place.

4. Make the wheels: colour a small quantity of sugar paste black and cut out 2 circles (or use 2 liquorice strips). Cut out 2 circles to fit inside them from grey sugar paste and mark out the pattern on the wheel hubs. Stick these on.

5. Use small portions of red, grey and black paste to make the rear lights, door handle, and window posts.

6. Use a food marker pen or a paintbrush dipped in diluted black gel colouring to paint in the back of the driver's seat.

pop-art flower biscuits

Sensational Party Cakes

Tip
If you don't have any gel colouring to hand or are in a hurry, you can decorate these biscuits even more simply, with piped white icing motifs, with or without silver sugar balls pressed into the icing before it sets.

ingredients for 15–20 biscuits
500 g uncooked biscuit mixture
  (see recipe on page 16)
400 g white royal icing
100 g plain chocolate or
  dark icing
rolling pin
pastry cutter
water-soluble gel colourings and
  a matching number of disposable
  piping bags (see method)

Make the biscuit mixture and roll it out with a rolling pin to a thickness of about 5 mm. Use a suitably shaped 4–5·cm pastry cutter to cut out the flower biscuits. Bake in a preheated oven at 180°C/gas mark 4 for 15–20 minutes until golden brown.

While the biscuits are cooling, make white royal icing (see pages 22 and 23). Pour equal amounts into as many bowls as your chosen colours and colour each batch. Cover the bowls at once with clingfilm. Fill each piping bag in turn with a colour and almost completely cover some of the biscuits, then repeat with the other piping bags and colours. Use melted chocolate or dark icing to pipe a little semicircle in the centre of each flower.

Everyone's a winner with this dice cake, which is decidedly unconventional but delicious and very easy to make.

dice cake

you will need
3 x 10-cm-square cakes about
  3 cm high
filling of your choice
  (see page 17)
200 g apricot jam
icing sugar, sifted
500 g white sugar paste
liquorice rounds
10 g white icing
pastry brush
rolling pin
pastry cutting wheel

Put one of the cakes on the serving plate, spread half the filling over it and place the second cake on top. Spread with the remaining filling and top with the third cake. You should have a cube-shaped cake. Microwave the apricot jam for 1 minute or heat for 3–4 minutes over hot water (push through a sieve once melted). Using a pastry brush, spread the cakes with a layer of warm jam.

1. Dust the work surface and rolling pin with icing sugar and roll the sugar paste out into a 4–5-mm thick sheet, large enough to cover the top and four sides of the cake.

2. Sprinkle the surface of the paste and the rolling pin with more icing sugar, roll the paste up around the rolling pin, then carefully unroll it to cover the cake completely. Take great care not to pull the sheet of sugar paste to avoid damaging the upper corners and the edges of the cake cube. Where the sugar paste falls in folds, these will need careful trimming and adjustment for a smooth finish. Using a pastry cutting wheel or a small sharp knife, cut off any excess sugar paste.

3. Use the liquid icing to stick the liquorice rounds on the top and sides of the dice as shown opposite.

Tip
A thick, rich and creamy filling is best for tall cakes like this one.

The harmony of shape, line and colour which epitomises the paintings of this great artist has inspired the design of this versatile cake.

Mondrian cake

you will need
1 x 20-cm square cake
200 g apricot jam
icing sugar, sifted
500 g white sugar paste
300 g caster sugar
red, yellow and blue
  water-soluble gel colouring
10–12 thin liquorice strips
100 g white royal icing
pastry brush
rolling pin
pastry cutting wheel
3 small freezer bags
3 cocktail sticks
ballpoint pen
greaseproof paper
piping bag

Place the cake on a serving plate. Microwave the apricot jam for 1 minute or heat for 3–4 minutes over hot water (push through a sieve once melted). Using a pastry brush, spread the cake with a layer of warm jam. Dust the work surface and rolling pin with icing sugar and roll the white sugar paste out into a 5–6·cm thick sheet, large enough to cover the cake, sides included. Sprinkle the surface of the paste and the rolling pin with more icing sugar, roll the paste up around the rolling pin, then carefully unroll it to cover the cake completely. Using a pastry cutting wheel or a small sharp knife, cut off any excess sugar paste.

1. Divide the caster sugar into 4 batches. Place 3 of these in 3 separate bags and use separate cocktail sticks to add a drop of different colouring to each of the bags. Add a drop of water and mix with the sugar by rubbing the bag with your fingers to colour evenly.

2. Draw the Mondrian design full-scale with a ballpoint pen on greaseproof paper. Hold this gently in place on top of the cake and prick out the design through the paper into the sugar paste with a pin. Trim the liquorice to the various lengths of all the lines, and stick these in place with royal icing, using a piping bag with a small nozzle.

3. Use a teaspoon to fill in the compartments with white and coloured sugar, pushing it into the corners with a cocktail stick.

A cake with a strikingly graphic design: the black-and-white scheme creates an illusion of movement reminiscent of abstract art, the perfect choice for a sophisticated friend.

op-art cake

you will need
1 x rectangular cake: 20 x 15 cm
200 g apricot jam
icing sugar, sifted
700 g white sugar paste
  (300 g of which to colour)
black water-soluble gel colouring
pastry brush
rolling pin
pastry cutting wheel
paintbrush

Place the cake on a serving plate. Microwave the apricot jam for 1 minute or heat for 3–4 minutes over hot water (push through a sieve once melted). Using a pastry brush, spread the cake with a layer of warm jam.

1. Dust the work surface and rolling pin with icing sugar, and roll 400 g of the white sugar paste out into a 4–5-cm thick sheet, large enough to cover the cake, sides included. Sprinkle the surface of the paste and the rolling pin with more icing sugar, roll the paste up around the rolling pin, then carefully unroll it to cover the cake completely. Using a pastry cutting wheel or a small sharp knife, cut off any excess sugar paste.

2. Colour the remaining 300 g sugar paste black; roll out and cut into strips of even width.

3. Cut the strips into 1.5-cm squares; you should have at least 70. Use a slightly moistened paintbrush to dampen and stick them to the cake as shown opposite. Trim the squares where necessary on the edges and corners. Use the edge of a very sharp knife, together with a ruler if necessary, to mark out parallel lines in the white sugar paste as illustrated.

An appetising way of playing 'he loves me, he loves me not', for someone who is mad about growing flowers and cooking, or for anyone who just loves a delicious and decorative treat.

sunflower cake

you will need
1 x 18-cm cake
200 g apricot jam
chocolate coating (see recipe
  on page 24)
30 g plain chocolate
2 red Smarties or M&Ms
200 g brown Smarties or M&Ms
1 x 17-cm cardboard disc
pastry brush
greaseproof paper
8 fresh flowers, e.g. gerberas
  or similar
cocktail sticks

Put the cake on the cardboard disc and place on a rack on top of a large plate. Microwave the apricot jam for 1 minute or heat for 3–4 minutes over hot water (push through a sieve once melted). Using a pastry brush, spread the cake with a layer of warm jam.

1. Make the chocolate coating and pour over the cake while still hot, making sure the sides are also completely covered. Leave to cool and set for a few minutes.

2. Melt the plain chocolate over hot water, transfer to a piping bag made of greaseproof paper, snip off the tip and pipe chocolate on to the red M&Ms to make the ladybirds.

3. Press the chocolate buttons or M&Ms lightly into the top of the cake in concentric circles, leaving 2 spaces: fill these with the ladybirds.

4. Just before serving, cut the stalks off the gerberas, slice the flower heads in half and surround the cake with them (see opposite). Use cocktail sticks, pushed into the thickest part of the flowers, to attach them to the cake if necessary.

prize allotment

Sensational Party Cakes

you will need
1 x rectangular cake: 25 x 15 cm
200 g apricot jam
700 g chocolate coating or melted
  chocolate or chocolate ganache
  (see recipes on page 24)
600 g almond paste or sugar paste
green and orange water-soluble
  gel colouring
green M&Ms
50 g plain chocolate
chocolate Matchsticks,
  trimmed to size, or chocolate
  finger biscuits
250 g muscovado sugar
1 x 24 x 14-cm rectangular
  cardboard cake base
pastry brush
cocktail sticks

Put the cake base under the cake and place on a rack on top of a very large plate. Microwave the apricot jam for 1 minute or heat for 3–4 minutes over hot water (push through a sieve once melted). Using a pastry brush, spread the cake with a layer of warm jam.

1. Make your chosen chocolate covering and coat the top and sides of the cake. Colour batches of almond paste or sugar paste in varying shades of green or orange, leaving some uncoloured.

2. Shape the vegetables. Baby carrots: shape the orange paste and make little grooves on them with the back of a small knife, then stick on tufts of green paste strips using a damp pastry brush.

Pumpkins: shape two slightly squashed balls, press the back of a knife down the sides and cut out leaves from the green paste. Press these lightly into place.

Peas: roll some green paste out and cut out the matching halves of pea pods. Place some green M&Ms on 1 half and place the other half on top.

Cabbages: shape small balls of uncoloured paste for the cabbage hearts; cut out leaves of varying sizes from light green and dark green paste and stick them together in concentric circles, attached to their slightly dampened hearts.

Turnips: shape fairly small, slightly squashed balls of uncoloured paste and press some very thin strips of green paste into their tops.

Leeks: roll strips of white and green paste around each other (see opposite) to form a cylinder. Insert a cocktail stick halfway into the base and secure the leeks vertically to the cake. Make the watering can with paste of a deeper orange.

3. Melt the plain chocolate over hot water, dip the chocolate Matchsticks into it and secure the 'fence' to the sides of the cake.

4. Sprinkle the sugar on to the cake in rows and place the vegetables on it.

frosted rosebud cake

Sensational Party Cakes

you will need
1 x 18-cm cake
200 g apricot jam
300 g white chocolate coating
** (see recipe on page 24)**
1 egg white, lightly whisked
100 g caster sugar
10 g white royal icing
1 x 17-cm cardboard disc
30 rosebuds, variegated orange
** or as desired**
pastry brush
60-cm length orange
** (or matching) ribbon**

Place the cake, on its cardboard disc, on a rack over a large plate. Microwave the apricot jam for 1 minute or heat for 3–4 minutes over hot water (push through a sieve once melted). Using a pastry brush, spread the cake with a layer of warm jam.

1. Make the white chocolate covering (using 400 g white chocolate and 25 g butter instead of the dark chocolate and rum). Pour all over the cake and when set, transfer to a serving plate.

2. Cut the rose stems very short. Dip each bud in egg white and sprinkle with the caster sugar. Insert the stems into the cake. Place the ribbon around the cake and secure the ends with royal icing.

black-and-white
biscuits

ingredients for 15–20 biscuits
500 g biscuit mixture
(see recipe on page 16)
200 g white royal icing
200 g plain chocolate
rolling pin
pastry cutter
2 disposable piping bags
cocktail sticks

Make the biscuit mixture. Roll it out with a rolling pin to a thickness of about 5 mm. Use a 5–6-mm pastry cutter or the rim of a small glass to cut out discs.

Make the royal icing, to 'ribbon' consistency (see page 23, liquid icing), and melt the chocolate over hot water. Fill one of the piping bags with the white royal icing and the other with the melted chocolate. Cover half the biscuits with white icing and the other half with chocolate, then decorate them with the contrasting colour: for the spider's web, draw concentric circles then, using a cocktail stick, drag out transversal lines; for the little hearts, pipe a series of small blobs in concentric circles then, using a cocktail stick, trace a line that links them all; for the little flowers, pipe a 5-petal flower then, using a cocktail stick, drag lines from each petal towards the centre of the biscuit.

A cake that puts one in mind of Nordic countries with its traditional Scandinavian motif, and is perfect as an easy introduction to cake decorating.

stamp motif cake

you will need
1 x 18-cm cake
200 g apricot jam
icing sugar, sifted
500 g sugar paste (100 g of which
  to colour red)
red water-soluble gel colouring
pastry brush
rolling pin
pastry cutting wheel
paintbrush
1 wooden or rubber stamp

Place the cake on a serving plate. Microwave the apricot jam for 1 minute or heat for 3–4 minutes over hot water (push through a sieve once melted). Using a pastry brush, spread the cake with a layer of warm jam.

1. Dust the work surface and rolling pin with icing sugar, then roll out 400 g of the white sugar paste to a thickness of 5–6 mm, large enough to cover the entire cake and its edges. Sprinkle the surface of the paste with more icing sugar, roll the paste up around the rolling pin, then carefully unroll it to cover the cake completely. Using a pastry cutting wheel or a small knife, cut off any excess sugar paste.

2. Colour about 100 g sugar paste red, roll it out with the rolling pin and cut out several strips. Pass a barely moistened small paintbrush over the strips and stick these all around the sides of the cake.

3. Dip a paintbrush into the red colouring gel and paint colour on to your stamp. With a steady hand, press the red-coloured stamp into the top of the cake. Continue to decorate the entire surface of the cake (or until your chosen motif is complete).

three-tier bonbon cake

Sensational Party Cakes

you will need

3 cakes: 22 cm, 18 cm and 14 cm
200 g apricot jam
icing sugar, sifted
1.6 kg sugar paste (400 g of which
  to colour)
brown water-soluble gel colouring
300 g royal icing (200 g of which
  to colour brown)
a few chocolate truffles
1 x 17–cm and 1 x 13–cm
  cardboard discs
pastry brush
rolling pin
pastry cutting wheel
2 fluted pastry cutters (1 small
  and 1 smaller)
paintbrush
piping bag with 2-mm nozzle

Place the small and middle cakes on to the cardboard discs and place the large cake on a serving plate. Microwave the apricot jam for 1 minute or heat for 3–4 minutes over hot water (push through a sieve once melted). Using a pastry brush, spread the largest cake with a layer of warm jam. Dust the work surface and rolling pin with icing sugar and roll the sugar paste out into a 3–4-mm thick sheet, large enough to cover the entire cake, sides included, reserving 400 g to colour brown. Sprinkle the surface of the paste and the rolling pin with more icing sugar, roll the

paste up around the rolling pin, then carefully unroll it to cover the cake completely. Using a pastry cutting wheel or a small sharp knife, cut off any excess sugar paste. Repeat this process for the other cakes. Place the smaller cakes on top of the largest cake following the technique described on page 21.

1. Colour about 400 g sugar paste brown and roll this out. Roll out a small amount of white sugar paste. Cut out 20 very small brown flowers and 20 smaller white flowers using the fluted pastry cutters; press the smaller flowers firmly into the centre of the larger brown ones. Use some of the royal icing to stick them all over the sides of the largest cake.

2. Using the pastry cutting wheel, cut out wide and narrow strips of brown sugar paste. Moisten the smallest cake with a paintbrush then stick the brown strips on top, alternating between wide and narrow ones. Cut off any excess sugar paste with a pastry cutting wheel or sharp knife. Colour the remaining royal icing brown.

3. To make the roses, roll out the remaining brown sugar paste and cut out 4 rectangles about 12 cm long and 4 cm high. Fold them in half lengthways without pressing on the fold and gently roll them up so as to create roses. Stick these to the top of the cake with brown royal icing.

4. Fill a piping bag with a small round nozzle with brown royal icing and draw arabesque shapes on the sides of the middle cake.

5. Finish the cake by applying the truffles, sticking them on with brown royal icing.

moo-cow cake 70, pony merry-
go-round 72, elk cupcakes 75,
butterfly 76, fire engine 78, beastie
biscuits 80, button biscuits 81,
penguin cupcakes 82, marine pool
cake 84, panda 86, Halloween
pumpkin 88

sensational
party cakes
for children and teenagers

moo-cow cake

you will need
1 x 18-cm cake
200 g apricot jam
icing sugar, sifted
600 g sugar paste (200 g of which
  to colour)
red and black water-soluble
  gel colouring
card
pastry brush
rolling pin
pastry cutting wheel
cocktail stick
paintbrush
small round pastry cutter

Copy the cow template (see page 124) on to a piece of card. Place the card template on the cake and, using a serrated knife held vertically, cut around the template then place the cake on a serving plate. Microwave the apricot jam for 1 minute or heat for 3–4 minutes over hot water (push through a sieve once melted). Using a pastry brush, spread the cake with a layer of warm jam.

1. Dust the work surface and rolling pin with icing sugar and roll about 350 g of the sugar paste out into a 4–5-mm thick sheet, large enough to cover the cake, sides included. Sprinkle the surface of the paste and the rolling pin with more icing sugar, roll the paste up around the rolling pin, then carefully unroll it to cover the cake completely. Using a pastry cutting wheel or a small sharp knife, cut off any excess sugar paste.

2. Make the legs and ears with white sugar paste. Position the ears at the top of the head, securing them with a cocktail stick. Dilute a drop of red gel colouring with a little water and paint the inside of each ear with a paintbrush. Attach the legs.

3. Colour about 150 g sugar paste pink, roll it out and cut out the face. Model the udder with the remaining pink paste; stick these on by moistening one of the surfaces with a damp paintbrush. Using a small round pastry cutter, mark out the nostrils and colour them lightly in red.

4. Colour the remaining sugar paste black and create the horns and the eyes.

5. Put a small amount of black gel colouring on a small plate, dilute it slightly with a wet paintbrush and paint the spots on the body.

A timeless amusement, a dessert with a soft creaminess at its centre... a celebration cake for a small child who is growing up.

pony merry-go-round

Sensational Party Cakes

you will need
For the cake
3 cakes: 1 x 22 cm and
   2 x 18 cm
filling of your choice
   (see page 17)
200 g apricot jam
1.5 kg white sugar paste
   (400 g of which to colour
   light blue, 200 g red, 150 g
   dark blue, 20 g green, 20 g yellow)
dark blue, red, green and yellow
   water-soluble gel colouring
icing sugar, sifted
6 liquorice strips
greaseproof paper
paintbrush
pastry brush
rolling pin
pastry cutting wheel
1 x 17-cm cardboard disc
wooden skewer
pastry cutter
paintbrush
cocktail stick

For the ponies
   200 g white royal icing
   400 g white liquid icing
   variously coloured gel food
   colourings

   To make the ponies: a few
days before you plan to serve the
cake make the ponies by reproducing
them from the pony template (see
page 119), using the decorating with icing technique
(see page 23).

   Allow them to dry out for 1 day, then, using a
paintbrush, colour them with gels diluted with a very
small amount of water. Leave them to dry once more.
Carefully peel off the ponies from the greaseproof paper
and set aside.

(continued on page 74)

To make the merry-go-round: cut the 22-cm cake in half, fill it with a filling of your choice and place on a serving plate. Microwave the apricot jam for 1 minute or heat for 3–4 minutes over hot water (push through a sieve once melted). Using a pastry brush, spread the cake with a layer of warm jam.

1. Colour 400 g of the sugar paste light blue with a couple of drops of blue colouring. Dust the work surface and rolling pin with icing sugar and roll the sugar paste out into a 3–4-mm thick sheet, large enough to cover the entire cake and its sides. Sprinkle the surface of the paste and the rolling pin with more icing sugar, roll the paste up around the rolling pin, then carefully unroll it to cover the larger cake completely. Using a pastry cutting wheel or a small sharp knife, cut off any excess sugar paste. Stack the smaller cakes on top of each other, with filling between them and place a cardboard disc underneath the lower layer. Glaze them with melted, sieved apricot jam and cover with a 3–4-cm-thick sheet of white sugar paste. Cut a small wooden skewer into 3 pieces and insert these, arranged in a triangle, in the centre of the large cake; use a little icing as glue. Place the covered stacked smaller cakes on top of the larger cake, ensuring they are well centred.

2. Colour 150 g of the sugar paste dark blue, roll it out, cut out small discs using a very small round pastry cutter and cut these in half. Stick these semicircles around the bottom of the larger cake.

3. Make the top of the merry-go-round separately. Using your hands, model a little of the remaining white sugar paste so as to form a small cone shape. Place on top of the cake, in the centre. Roll out more paste and cut out a disc for the merry-go-round canopy. Stick this on to the top of the cake using a little icing.

4. Colour 200 g sugar paste red and cut out a disc as wide as the canopy. Cut out triangles from it and stick these on to the canopy, alternating red and white strips, using either a dampened paintbrush or a small amount of icing.

5. Stick the liquorice strips upright against the sides of the smaller cake, using icing, positioning them under the red canopy strips. Using a small pastry cutter, cut out red and white circles, cut them in half and stick these halves around the edge of the canopy.

6. Colour a small amount of sugar paste green and make a little flag. Fix this on to a cocktail stick and position at the very top of the canopy, finishing off with a small ball of yellow sugar paste.

7. Lastly, spread a little icing on the underside of each pony and very carefully attach them to the merry-go-round, pressing gently on the liquorice strips for a few seconds in order to make them stick.

Tip
As this cake is rather time-consuming to build up, you could, as an alternative, omit the making of the sugar ponies and use little figures cut out and pasted on to card instead. These should also be applied with a little icing.

elk cupcakes

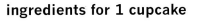

ingredients for 1 cupcake
1 cupcake (see recipe on page 15)
1 individual shop-bought rectangular
  chocolate sponge cake
300 g royal icing
brown water-soluble gel colouring
1 large piece candied lemon peel
  or ice cream wafer
small chocolate buttons
1 red M&M or 1 glacé cherry
small palette knife
3 cocktail sticks

1. Make the cupcake. Colour the icing brown and use a small palette knife to spread it over the cupcake.

2. Place the cupcake on the work surface and insert 3 cocktail sticks, arranged in a triangle, in the centre.

3. Trim off the sharp edges and corners of the individual chocolate sponge cake, tapering at one end to make the head, then attach this horizontally, pushing it on to the sticks. Cover the chocolate sponge cake with brown icing.

4. Cut out the elk's antlers from the candied peel or wafer; attach the peel to the head with a cocktail stick or push the wafer pieces into the head. Stick on the chocolate buttons for the eyes, and the red M&M or glacé cherry for the nose. Repeat as necessary to make more cupcakes.

A beautiful confection, ready to take flight, very suitable for a dreamy young girl who would not be content with just any old cake.

butterfly

you will need
1 x 18-cm cake
200 g apricot jam
icing sugar, sifted
800 g sugar paste or almond paste
   (300 g of which to colour pink and
   100 g black)
red and black water-soluble gel
   colouring
2 liquorice rounds
pastry brush
rolling pin
pastry cutting wheel
2 scalloped pastry cutters (1 large
   and 1 small)
paintbrush

Cut the cake in half and separate the 2 halves. Microwave the apricot jam for 1 minute or heat for 3–4 minutes over hot water (push through a sieve once melted). Using a pastry brush, spread the cake halves, which will form the butterfly's wings, with warm jam. Dust the work surface and rolling pin with icing sugar and roll 400 g of the uncoloured paste out into a 3–4-mm thick sheet, large enough to cover the 2 halves, sides included. Sprinkle the surface of the paste with more icing sugar, roll the paste up around the rolling pin, then carefully unroll it to cover one of the wings completely. Using a pastry cutting wheel or a small sharp knife, cut off any excess sugar paste. Repeat the process for the other wing.

1. Use the red colouring gel to colour 300 g of the paste pink, roll 100 g out and cut out several large and small flowers. Colour the remaining 100 g paste black and cut out more flowers. Dampening the surfaces with a wet paintbrush, stick the large flowers on to the wings, and the small flowers on top of the large ones.

2. Using the remaining pink paste, model out a cylinder shape for the body and head and decorate the body with tiny strips of black paste. Add the eyes then attach 2 unrolled liquorice rounds to the head. Assemble the body and wings on the serving plate.

fire engine

Sensational Party Cakes

you will need
3 rectangular cakes: 10 x 15 cm
  (or 1 large cake, cut into 3 slabs)
400 g confectioner's custard (see
  recipe on page 17) or jam of your
  choice, for filling
200 g apricot jam
1 kg sugar paste
icing sugar, sifted
red and black water-soluble
  gel colouring
yellow, brown and red M&Ms
liquorice rounds and strips
pastry brush
rolling pin
pastry cutting wheel
2 cocktail sticks

Place one of the cakes on a serving plate and fill it with a confectioner's custard or jam or your choice. Lay the second cake on top, fill this also and finally lay the third cake on top of this.

1. Shape the cabin: shave a thin, slanting piece from one end of the cake block (the 'front' of the fire engine, stopping halfway down this 'front end' of the cake. Then, starting from the 'back end', cut off a long, horizontal slice from the cake's top, about 1 cm in depth and two thirds of its length, leaving one third at the 'front' intact and higher for the cabin roof. Shape the sides and rear of the fire engine.

2. Microwave the apricot jam for 1 minute or heat for 3–4 minutes over hot water (push through a sieve once melted). Using a pastry brush, spread the third cake with a thin layer of warm jam.

3. Set aside about 100 g sugar paste for the white and grey parts and colour the remaining sugar paste red. Dust the work surface and rolling pin with icing sugar and roll the red sugar paste out into a 3–4-mm thick sheet, large enough to cover the entire cake, sides included. Take care not to damage the corners and edges of the cake. Using a pastry cutting wheel or a small sharp knife, cut off any excess sugar paste.

4. Roll out the reserved white sugar paste and model out the windscreen and two side windows. Dampen these slightly and fix on to the fire engine.

5. Using the black colouring, colour the remaining sugar paste grey, roll it out and shape the headlights, the registration plate, the bell, bumpers, radiator and water nozzles. Dampen the surface of the cake and stick these on. Shape the rear-view mirrors and fix them in place with the help of 2 cocktail sticks. Use yellow and red M&Ms for the lights. Attach 4 liquorice rounds for the wheels and stick a brown M&M in the centre of each. Shape the mudguards using the red sugar paste off-cuts. Attach a partially unrolled liquorice round on each side for the hoses. Use the liquorice strips to make the ladder, using white icing sugar to affix all these pieces

Tip
For a simpler version, cut out the cake using the template on page 120 with a serrated knife then decorate as above.

beastie
biscuits

ingredients for 20–25 biscuits
500 g biscuit mixture
  (see recipe on page 16)
300 g white royal icing
200 g plain chocolate
assorted sweets
rolling pin
pastry cutter
2 disposable piping bags
1 medium nozzle (for the icing),
  1 small nozzle (for the chocolate)

Make the biscuit mixture. Roll it out with a rolling pin to a thickness of about 5 mm and cut out discs using a 5–6-mm pastry cutter or the rim of a glass. Bake in a preheated oven at 180ºC/gas mark 4 for about 15–20 minutes until golden brown then leave to cool. The biscuits can also be made with puff pastry, or you can use smooth shop-bought biscuits.

2. Prepare the royal icing to 'ribbon' consistency (see page 23, liquid icing) and melt the chocolate over hot water. Fill 1 piping bag with white icing and the other with melted chocolate. Pipe the white icing over the biscuits so as to cover the surface entirely.

3. While the icing is still soft and sticky, decorate the biscuits with the sweets in order to form the insects' bodies, and draw in the legs and the antennae with the melted chocolate.

button biscuits

ingredients for 20–25 biscuits
500 g biscuit mixture (see recipe on
** page 16)**
400 g white royal icing
assorted water-soluble gel colourings
hundreds-and-thousands, chocolate
** vermicelli or sprinkles of your**
** choice, for decoration**
10 g coloured sugar
rolling pin
pastry cutter
1 plastic straw
disposable piping bags (as many as
** the colours you use)**

Make the biscuit mixture. Roll it out with a rolling pin to a
thickness of about 5 mm then cut out 5–6-mm discs with a
pastry cutter or the rim of a glass. Use a plastic straw to make
2 or 4 holes in each button biscuit. Bake in a preheated oven
at 180°C/gas mark 4 for about 15–20 minutes until golden
brown then leave to cool. Prepare the royal icing to 'ribbon'
consistency (see page 23, liquid icing) and divide it between
as many saucers as the colours you plan to use. Colour
each batch of icing with a different colour. Cover the saucers
immediately with clingfilm so the icing does not harden. Fill
each piping bag with a different coloured icing and cover the
biscuits, leaving the holes visible. Decorate the biscuits with
your chosen sprinkles while the icing is still fresh.

penguin cupcakes

ingredients for 1 cupcake
1 cupcake (see recipe on page 15)
1 individual shop-bought rectangular
  sponge cake
300 g royal icing
black water-soluble gel colouring
white and yellow marshmallows
white or yellow M&Ms
liquorice rounds
small palette knife
3 cocktail sticks
black food marker pen

1. Make the cupcake. Using a small spreader or palette knife, cover the cupcake with black icing, using circular movements for smooth, even coverage. Place the cupcake on the work surface and insert 3 cocktail sticks, arranged in a triangle, in the centre.

2. To make the penguin's head, cut off a piece of the sponge cake and make sure it is in proportion with the cupcake 'body'; round off the corners where necessary then push it on to the cocktail sticks to complete the penguin shape. Cover this also with black icing.

3. With a sharp knife, cut a thin slice of white marshmallow and stick it on to the cupcake to make the penguin's tummy. Cut a piece of yellow marshmallow and create the beak and the feet.

4. Stick the beak on, pressing gently on the still-soft icing to ensure it adheres. Thread the 'feet' on to the tips of cocktail sticks and insert these into the bottom of the cupcake. Stick the M&Ms into the face to make the eyes, drawing the pupils with a black food marker pen. Finally, cut a liquorice round in half and stick both halves on to the penguin to make the flippers. Repeat as necessary to make more cupcakes.

Tip
The food marker pen, which is very useful in this kind of decorative work, is available in specialised food shops and from cake decorating suppliers on the internet. Skilled cake decorators can create the snowflakes shown with icing, working it on a marble slab or non-stick paper and using a cocktail stick in order to 'pull' and model it. Once dry, these decorations will be quite fragile but can be handled with care.

marine pool cake

you will need

For the cake

1 x 22-cm cake
200 g apricot jam
700 g sugar paste (of which 400 g to colour light blue, 150 g dark blue, 100 g red, 50 g white)
blue and red water-soluble gel colouring
icing sugar, sifted
pastry brush
rolling pin
pastry cutting wheel

For the fishes

50 g plain chocolate
50 g milk chocolate
150 g white chocolate
red, dark blue and yellow fat-soluble colouring
greaseproof paper

For the fishes: see decorating with chocolate on page 25.

For the cake: place the cake on a serving plate. Microwave the apricot jam for 1 minute or heat for 3–4 minutes over hot water (push through a sieve once melted). Using a pastry brush, spread the cake with a layer of warm jam.

1. Colour 400 g sugar paste light blue. Dust the work surface and rolling pin with icing sugar and roll the sugar paste out into a 4–5-mm thick sheet, large enough to cover the entire cake, sides included. Sprinkle the surface of the paste with more icing sugar, roll the paste up around the rolling pin, then carefully unroll it to cover the cake completely. Using a pastry cutting wheel or a small sharp knife, cut off any excess sugar paste.

2. Colour 150 g sugar paste dark blue, roll it out 4–5 mm thick and cut out a strip as wide as the side of the cake is high and long enough to stretch all round the cake. Dampen the sides of the cake with a pastry brush and stick the dark blue strip in place.

3. Colour 100 g sugar paste red and make a thin sausage shape about 1 cm thick and the same length as the dark blue strip. Dampen the upper edge of the cake and affix the red sausage shape (with the join in the same place as the dark blue strip). Using the white sugar paste, model out a life-ring and decorate this as shown with the red sugar paste. Stick the fishes to the surface with a little white icing.

This is a cake that is inspired by the black eye make-up favoured by many a teenage girl, as well as being a tribute to one of the world's best-loved animals.

panda

Sensational Party Cakes

you will need
1 x 18-cm cake
200 g apricot jam
icing sugar, sifted
600 g sugar paste (200 g of which
  to colour black)
black water-soluble gel colouring
greaseproof paper
card
pastry brush
rolling pin
pastry cutting wheel

Trace the panda template (see page 121) using greaseproof paper and transfer it on to card. Lay the card template on the cake and, using a serrated knife held vertically, cut out the panda shape. Place the cake on a serving plate. Microwave the apricot jam for 1 minute or heat for 3–4 minutes over hot water (push through a sieve once melted). Using a pastry brush, spread the cake with a layer of warm jam.

1. Dust the work surface and rolling pin with icing sugar and roll 400 g sugar paste out into a 4–5-mm thick sheet, large enough to cover the cake, sides included. Sprinkle the surface of the paste with more icing sugar, roll the paste up around the rolling pin, then carefully unroll it to cover the cake completely. Using a pastry cutting wheel or a small sharp knife, cut off any excess sugar paste.

2. Colour the remaining sugar paste black, roll it out rather thickly and model the 2 ears. Dampen the surface of the cake slightly and stick these on, securing them if necessary with a cocktail stick. Model the eyes and the nose in black. Dilute a little black food colouring in a small plate and, using a paintbrush, paint on the mouth starting from the centre of the nose.

Halloween pumpkin

you will need
1 x 18-cm cake
200 g apricot jam
600 g almond paste (400 g of which
   to colour orange, 100 g green,
   75 g black, 25 g uncoloured)
orange, green and black
   water-soluble gel colouring
icing sugar, sifted
greaseproof paper
card
pastry brush
rolling pin
pastry cutting wheel
paintbrush

Trace the pumpkin template on greaseproof paper and transfer it on to card. Lay this on top of the cake. Using a serrated knife held vertically, cut out the pumpkin shape, then place the cake on a serving plate. Microwave the apricot jam for 1 minute or heat for 3–4 minutes over hot water (push through a sieve once melted). Using a pastry brush, spread the cake with a layer of warm jam.

1. Colour 400 g of the almond paste orange. Dust the work surface and rolling pin with icing sugar and roll the paste out into a 5–6-mm thick sheet, large enough to cover the cake, sides included. Sprinkle the surface of the almond paste with more icing sugar, roll the paste up around the rolling pin, then carefully unroll it to cover the cake completely. Press your fingers into the almond paste, making shallow grooves and depressions to create a pumpkin-skin effect. Using a pastry cutting wheel or a small sharp knife, cut off any excess sugar paste.

2. Colour 100 g almond paste with a few drops of green food colouring, then roll it out thinly with the rolling pin. Cut out leaf shapes and place these at the top of the cake. Make small strips out of the green almond paste, roll them up a little and apply them here and there, to suggest tendrils.

3. Colour 75 g almond paste black, roll it out and cut out 3 triangles: 2 for the pumpkin's eyes and 1 for the nose. Using a small knife, cut out a serrated, irregular mouth shape. Moisten a paintbrush and dampen the surface of the cake before applying all these features. Cut out 2 circles from the remaining uncoloured almond paste to use as pupils for the pumpkin's eyes.

sensational party cakes

for celebrations

gift-wrapped cake

you will need
3 x 10-cm square cakes about
   3 cm high
confectioner's custard (see recipe
   on page 17) or jam, for filling
200 g apricot jam
700 g sugar paste or almond paste
   (500 g of which to colour red)
red water-soluble gel colouring
icing sugar, sifted
50 g white icing
pastry brush
rolling pin
pastry cutting wheel
clingfilm

Place one of the cakes on a serving plate and spread it with plenty of confectioner's custard or jam. Place the second cake on top of the first one, spread with more filling, then lay the third cake on top of this. Microwave the apricot jam for 1 minute or heat for 3–4 minutes over hot water (push through a sieve once melted). Using a pastry brush, spread the cake with a layer of warm jam.

1. Colour 500 g of the sugar paste or almond paste red, reserving 200 g of uncoloured paste to make the ribbon. Dust the work surface and rolling pin with icing sugar and roll the paste out into a 4–5·mm thick sheet, large enough to cover the entire cake, sides included. Sprinkle the surface of the paste with more icing sugar, roll the paste up around the rolling pin, then carefully unroll it to cover the cake completely. Take care not to damage the corners and edges of the cake. Using a pastry cutting wheel or a small sharp knife, cut off any excess paste.

2. To make the lid (optional), make a strip out of the red sugar paste or almond paste, gently roll it up without damaging it, then dampen the upper part of the gift box's sides. Apply the strip all around the box to look like the lid's side. Cut out a square to match the uppermost surface of the cake, dampen this surface, then join the edges of the square with the lid's sides.

3. Roll the uncoloured paste out and cut strips to suggest a ribbon tied round the box. Model the bow in the ribbon, inserting some rolled up clingfilm inside the loops so they keep their shape while drying. When dry, stick the bow on to the top of the box, using the white icing.

A cake that enables you to personalise the recipient's age, perfect for a celebration of the milestone eighteenth birthday.

T-shirt cake

you will need
1 x 22-cm cake
200 g apricot jam
500 g sugar paste
orange water-soluble gel colouring
icing sugar, sifted
blue Smarties
greaseproof paper
card
pastry brush
rolling pin
pastry cutting wheel
paintbrush
kitchen string
wooden pegs

Use greaseproof paper to trace the T-shirt template (see page 125) and transfer it on to card. Place this template on the cake and cut out the T-shirt shape, using a serrated knife held vertically, taking care not to squash the cake and to achieve a smooth cut. Microwave the apricot jam for 1 minute or heat for 3–4 minutes over hot water (push through a sieve once melted). Using a pastry brush, spread the cake with a layer of warm jam.

1. Colour the sugar paste orange, reserving a small amount to model the number on the T-shirt. Dust the work surface and rolling pin with icing sugar and roll the sugar paste out into a 3–4-mm thick sheet, large enough to cover the cake, sides included. Sprinkle the surface of the paste with more icing sugar, roll the paste up around the rolling pin, then carefully unroll it to cover the cake completely. Using a pastry cutting wheel or a small sharp knife, cut off any excess sugar paste.

2. Colour the remaining small amount of sugar paste if you wish, roll it out with the rolling pin, cut out the relevant numbers and dampen the surface of the cake where they are to go with a paintbrush dipped in water. Stick the number on to the T-shirt and position the Smarties as shown. Complete the cake by arranging a length of kitchen string on top and positioning some pegs to suggest a washing line.

An easy but effective cake to mark an amusing occasion; suitable for children or for grown-ups who still like to play.

family tree cake

Sensational Party Cakes

you will need
1 x 18-cm cake
200 g apricot jam
icing sugar, sifted
700 g white sugar paste (150 g of
 which to colour)
pink, brown, black, yellow and red
 water-soluble gel colouring
pink or red heart-shaped sweets
a few real leaves
pastry brush
rolling pin
pastry cutting wheel
ricer
scissors
paintbrush
cocktail stick or food marker pen

Place the cake on the serving plate. Microwave the apricot jam for 1 minute or heat for 3–4 minutes over hot water (push through a sieve once melted). Using a pastry brush, spread the cake with a layer of warm jam.

1. Dust the work surface and rolling pin with icing sugar and roll 400 g of the sugar paste out into a 4–5-mm thick sheet, large enough to cover the entire cake, sides included. Sprinkle the surface of the paste with more icing sugar, roll the paste up around the rolling pin, then carefully unroll it to cover the cake completely. Using a pastry cutting wheel or a small sharp knife, cut off any excess sugar paste.

(continued on page 98)

2. Colour about 150 g sugar paste pale pink in order to model the faces and also colour small amounts of sugar paste in the other colours you need to complete them. Wrap the sugar paste balls in clingfilm so they don't dry out.

3. To make the faces, cut out as many circles in pink sugar paste as the people you want to appear on the cake. Use brown sugar paste for the dog.

4. To make the hair, push coloured sugar paste through a ricer and cut with a small knife. Dampen the upper border of the pink circles and apply the hair, trimming it if necessary with a small pair of scissors.

5. Create the other details (the hat, bib, spectacles, beard, moustache and so on) with coloured sugar paste and stick these on, using a dampened paintbrush.

6. Mark out the eyes by dipping the end of a cocktail stick in coloured gel or with a food marker pen.

7. Dampen the surface of the faces and stick on the heart-shaped sweets for the ladies' mouths. Using a damp, fine paintbrush dipped in colour, outline the mouths of the male figures and children.

8. For the tree, dilute a little brown gel with a few drops of water in a small saucer and use a paintbrush to draw the trunk and branches on the surface of the cake. Stick the various faces in position, using a damp paintbrush. Finally, place the leaves here and there as you wish.

Sensational Party Cakes

Tip
Be careful with your choice of colouring: water-soluble gel colouring is suitable for sugar paste as well as for almond paste and icing. Powder and liquid colouring, on the other hand, are used only for icing. For chocolate, use fat-soluble colouring.

little men
biscuits

ingredients for 15–20 biscuits
400 g biscuit mixture (see recipe
  on page 16)
100 g royal icing
a few silver sugar balls
gingerbread man pastry cutter
piping bag

  Roll out the biscuit mixture until it is
about ½ cm then cut out the little men with
a pastry cutter or a knife. Bake the biscuits
in a preheated oven at 180°C/gas mark 4
for about 15–20 minutes until golden brown
then allow to cool. Fill a piping bag with
icing and decorate the biscuits with icing
and silver balls as you wish.

horror
biscuits

ingredients for 15–20 biscuits
400 g biscuit mixture (see recipe
  on page 16)
200 g apricot jam

  Roll out the biscuit mixture until it is
about ½ cm then cut out an even number
of discs about 4–5 cm in diameter. Spread
the jam over half the discs, cut out eyes
and mouths in the remaining discs, then
stick the 2 halves together. Bake the
biscuits in a preheated oven at 180°C/gas
mark 4 for about 15–20 minutes until
golden brown.

Make someone's dreams come true with this heart-shaped cake. There are a thousand occasions that justify baking one, so just find the right one and savour a moment of pure magic.

heart-shaped cake

Sensational Party Cakes

you will need
1 x 22-cm cake, baked in a heart-
   shaped tin
200 g apricot jam
500 g almond paste
red water-soluble gel colouring
icing sugar, sifted
100 g white royal icing
pastry brush
rolling pin
pastry cutting wheel
piping bag

Place the cake on a serving plate. Microwave the apricot jam for 1 minute or heat for 3–4 minutes over hot water (push through a sieve once melted). Using a pastry brush, spread the cake with a layer of warm jam.

1. Colour the almond paste red. Dust the work surface and rolling pin with icing sugar and roll the almond paste out into a 5–6-mm thick sheet, large enough to cover the cake and its sides. Sprinkle the surface of the paste and the rolling pin with more icing sugar, roll the paste up around the rolling pin, then carefully unroll it to cover the cake completely. Using a pastry cutting wheel or a small sharp knife, cut off any excess sugar paste.

2. Dilute some lukewarm apricot jam with just a little water and spread it very sparingly all over the almond paste-decorated cake to achieve a shiny effect. Allow the jam to cool and set (see Tip, page 20).

3. When the glaze on the cake has dried and set, fit a narrow round nozzle in the piping bag and fill the bag with white icing. Pipe a grid made up of parallel and perpendicular lines, leaving an empty border of about 2 cm all around. Draw little hearts on the border.

Making and then sampling these snowman cupcakes is enough excuse to throw a winter party; have fun giving each snowman a different face.

snowman cupcakes

ingredients for 1 cupcake
1 large and 1 small cupcake
(see recipe on page 15)
300 g white royal icing
chocolate buttons or black sweets,
for the eyes
Smarties or M&Ms, pastilles, red
and black liquorice rounds and
strips, custard cream biscuits
small palette knife
cocktail sticks

Make the cupcakes. Using a small palette knife, cover the larger cupcake with icing, using circular movements to ensure the icing is applied smoothly. Place the cupcake on the work surface and insert 3 cocktail sticks, arranged in a triangle, in the centre. Secure the smaller cupcake on these, at an angle, to represent the snowman's head (see page 21), and coat this second cupcake with icing. Decorate the snowman by positioning the chocolate buttons or black sweets for the eyes, then use Smarties, M&Ms, pastilles, liquorice rounds and strips and biscuits as you like to make up the other features of the snowman. Should the icing have hardened too much, secure the features with some leftover white icing.

Tip
As the cupcakes are small, the snowman version is shown off to best advantage if served as a series; a single one does not have such a dramatic effect. For maximum impact, make several snowmen and decorate them in as varied a way as possible.

flowery meadow

you will need
1 x 22-cm cake
600 g sugar paste
green, black and yellow
    water-soluble gel colouring
1 leaf gelatine
1 rice noodle
200 g apricot jam
icing sugar, sifted
10 g white icing
cocktail stick
paintbrush
rolling pin
flower-shaped pastry cutter
pastry brush
pastry cutting wheel
black food marker pen
clingfilm

Make the bee and daisies at least
12 hours in advance. Colour 120 g of
the sugar paste yellow.

1. For the bee, form a small cylinder for
the body and a small ball for the head with
about two thirds of the yellow sugar paste.
Attach the head to the body with the aid of
a cocktail stick. Using a paintbrush, draw
stripes on the body and take care not to
touch them with your fingers. With a small
paper template, cut out 2 wings from the
gelatine leaf then insert them into the body
before it sets and hardens. Dip a couple of
pieces of the rice noodle into a small amount of black
gel colouring to make the antennae and insert these
into the head.

2. For the daisies, roll out about 80 g of the white
sugar paste and cut out 2 flower shapes with a flower-
shaped pastry cutter; alternatively, cut out the flower
with a small sharp knife. Allow each flower to dry on
a support or on scrunched-up clingfilm, to prevent
the petals from drooping. Shape 2 little balls with the
remaining yellow paste then flatten them, pressing them
gently against a grater for a patterned effect. Dampen
the surface of each set of petals slightly and stick the
yellow centres in the middle. Leave the bee and daisies
to dry for at least 12 hours.

3. Place the cake on a serving plate. Microwave the
apricot jam for 1 minute or heat for 3–4 minutes over
hot water (push through a sieve once melted). Using a
pastry brush, spread the cake with a layer of warm jam.

4. Colour the remaining sugar paste light green.
Dust the work surface and rolling pin with icing sugar
and roll the sugar paste out into a 3–4-mm thick sheet,
large enough to cover the entire cake, sides included.
Sprinkle the surface of the paste with more icing sugar,
roll the paste up around the rolling pin, then carefully
unroll it to cover the cake completely. Using a pastry
cutting wheel or a small sharp knife, cut off any excess
sugar paste. Arrange the 2 daisies and the bee on top of
the cake, securing them with a little white icing. Using
a black food marker pen, draw a row of Zs on top of
the cake, to suggest the buzzing of the bee. You could
complete the cake by tying a matching ribbon around it.

A huge chocolate egg with a soft centre, embellished with mouth-watering icings; decorate it lavishly according to your own fancy.

Easter egg

you will need
1 x 22-cm cake
200 g apricot jam
700 g chocolate coating
 (see page 24)
200 g royal icing
water-soluble gel colouring in
 colours of your choice
200 g sugar paste
cardboard cake base
pastry brush
piping bags (as many as the colours
 you use)
clingfilm

Bake the cake of your choice in an Easter egg cake tin or, alternatively, draw an egg template on a piece of card, cut it out and lay it on top of the cake. Using a serrated knife held vertically, cut out the egg shape. With the serrated knife, trim the cake into an egg shape. Place it on a cardboard cake base a little smaller than the cake, and place this on a cooling rack, over a serving plate. Microwave the apricot jam for 1 minute or heat for 3–4 minutes over hot water (push through a sieve once melted). Using a pastry brush, spread the cake with a layer of warm jam.

1. Make the chocolate coating and pour this over the cake. Leave to dry.

2. Colour the royal icing with colours of your choice, then fill each piping bag with a different colour icing. Decorate the cake as you like by piping the decoration with the coloured icings.

3. Colour the sugar paste orange and cut out a strip to make the bow; insert some rolled-up clingfilm inside the bow's loops to keep their shape as it dries. Finally, lay the bow on top of the Easter egg.

Santa Claus on skis

you will need
1 tall, shop-bought Pandoro, sweet
  yeast, or sponge, cake
400 g sugar paste
red, green, brown and black water-
  soluble gel colouring
icing sugar, sifted
cocktail sticks
black food marker pen

Cut through the cake with a serrated knife to create a gradient of about 30 degrees (see illustration opposite). Place on a serving plate.

1. To make the Santa Claus figure, colour a little sugar paste brown and roll it out thinly. Cut out 2 short and narrow rectangles to make the skis and curve the tips slightly upwards. Colour part of the remaining sugar paste red and model a slightly flattened ball to make the body and two cylinders to make the arms. Dampen the surface slightly and stick the arms on to the body.

2. Flatten the lower extremities of the arms in order to make the gloves. Finally, prepare two small sausage shapes for the legs and a small cone to stick on to the head by way of a hat. Colour a small ball of sugar paste pink and make the face (reserve a very small amount of this to make the nose) and attach it to the body with a piece of cocktail stick. Mark out the eyes using the black food marker pen. For the boots, colour a little sugar paste black, model 2 short sausage shapes, fold them into an 'L' shape and stick them below the legs.

3. With the white sugar paste make the edges of the sleeves and hat, the moustache, the pompom on the hat and the beard. Dampen the surface slightly and stick all these features on. With the aid of a few cocktail sticks, secure Santa Claus, on his skis, on the slope of the cake. For the ski poles, put a small round of brown sugar paste on to the tips of 2 cocktail sticks.

4. To make the tree, colour the remaining sugar paste green and model a long sausage shape about 1 cm in diameter. Cut this in ½-cm long segments then shape these into cones and use them to build up the tree on the serving plate. Sprinkle sifted icing sugar over the cake to simulate snow.

A fairy-tale cake suitable for winter teatimes, enlivened by tasty little biscuits that will appeal to youngsters.

Hansel and Gretel's house

Sensational Party Cakes

you will need

1 shop-bought Panettone sweet yeast cake
900 g raw biscuit mixture (see recipe and quantities on page 16)
300 g royal icing
brown and red water-soluble gel colouring
paper
greaseproof paper
rolling pin
piping bag and round nozzle

Measure the Panettone's circumference and divide this by 6 or 7, so as to calculate the measurement for the width of each biscuit house façade with which you will decorate the cake.

1. Draw the houses on a sheet of paper (using the templates on pages 122 and 123) and cut these out; their total length needs to be slightly greater than the Panettone's circumference.

2. Place a sheet of greaseproof paper on a marble slab or work surface, and roll the biscuit mixture out into a 6–7-mm thick sheet. Lay the templates on top of the biscuit mixture and cut out the house façades using a sharp knife. Bake in a preheated oven at 180°C/ gas mark 4 for about 15–20 minutes until lightly browned and allow to cool.

3. Colour 100 g of the icing brown, cover and set aside. Use the remaining white icing to decorate the biscuit houses with a piping bag and a round nozzle. Leave to dry for about 10 minutes. Shape the sides of the Panettone with a serrated knife to ensure that each biscuit house fits snugly.

4. Stick each biscuit house on to the Panettone using brown icing; press gently for a few seconds to ensure they stick well. Finally, mix the remaining brown icing with red gel colouring and, using the piping bag, draw the roof tiles on top of the cake.

Little edible table decorations or sweet gifts that are original and unique treats for friends who will appreciate the effort you have made.

Christmas tree
cupcakes

you will need
1 large cupcake and 1 small one
(see recipe on page 15)
300 g royal icing
green water-soluble gel colouring
about 30 multi-coloured Smarties
or M&Ms
piping bag with star nozzle
3 cocktail sticks

1. Make the cupcakes. Colour the royal icing green using the gel and mix it thoroughly. Fill a piping bag fitted with a star nozzle with the icing.

2. Cover the entire surface of the larger cupcake with the icing, piping elongated, slightly drooping rosettes in concentric circles, starting off with the outermost circle. Ensure that the rosettes of icing are pointing outwards and downwards.

3. Place the iced cupcake on the work surface, leave the icing to set a little then insert three cocktail sticks, arranged in a triangle, in the centre; push the smaller cupcake on to these so that it sits on top of the larger cupcake. Ice the smaller cupcake in the same way as the larger one, ending with an icing tip pointing upwards.

4. While the icing is still soft, stick on the Smarties or M&Ms to decorate the cupcakes.

Tip
Place a Christmas cupcake next to every place setting on the festive table; at the end of the meal, each guest will have a sweet treat to eat, or to take home as a favour.

These are an extra-sweet variation on the more traditional Christmas baubles but are not hung on the tree; they are suitable as gifts or as a centrepiece for the table.

Christmas baubles

Sensational Party Cakes

you will need
1 cupcake for each Christmas bauble
   (see recipe on page 15)
200 g white royal icing
M&Ms or Smarties and pastilles
red and black liquorice rounds
   and strips
coloured and silver sugar balls
chocolate vermicelli
coloured sugars, edible rainbow dust
small palette knife
piping bag with a 3-mm nozzle
paintbrush

1. Make the cupcakes. Using a small palette knife, cover each cupcake with icing, using circular movements to ensure the icing is applied smoothly. Place the iced cupcakes on the work surface and decorate them as you wish using M&Ms or Smarties, pastilles, liquorice rounds and strips, sugar balls, chocolate vermicelli, coloured sugars and rainbow dust. Should the icing harden too much, you can stick the larger decorations on with some leftover white icing, using a small brush or a cocktail stick. More skilled cake decorators can create small figures with icing using a piping bag with a 3-mm nozzle, piping out each figure in relief directly on to each bauble. The finished figures can then be painted with a paintbrush.

2. The final touch that makes these Christmas baubles all the more realistic is the black 'hook'; this is created using a small length of liquorice strip, stuck on with a dot of icing on top of each cupcake, and completed by a small black circle, curled up like a ring made with a piece cut from a liquorice round. If you plan to use coloured sugars, chocolate vermicelli or edible rainbow dust, sprinkle them over the icing while this is still soft. Leave the cupcakes to dry and present the finished product at an angle, as shown in the photograph opposite, to hide the paper cases.

sensational party cakes

templates

the templates on the following pages are, in so far as is possible, drawn to actùal size and are therefore suitable for making the cake in the dimensions specified in each recipe.

handbag cake page 36

fluttering butterflies page 42

platform shoe page 38

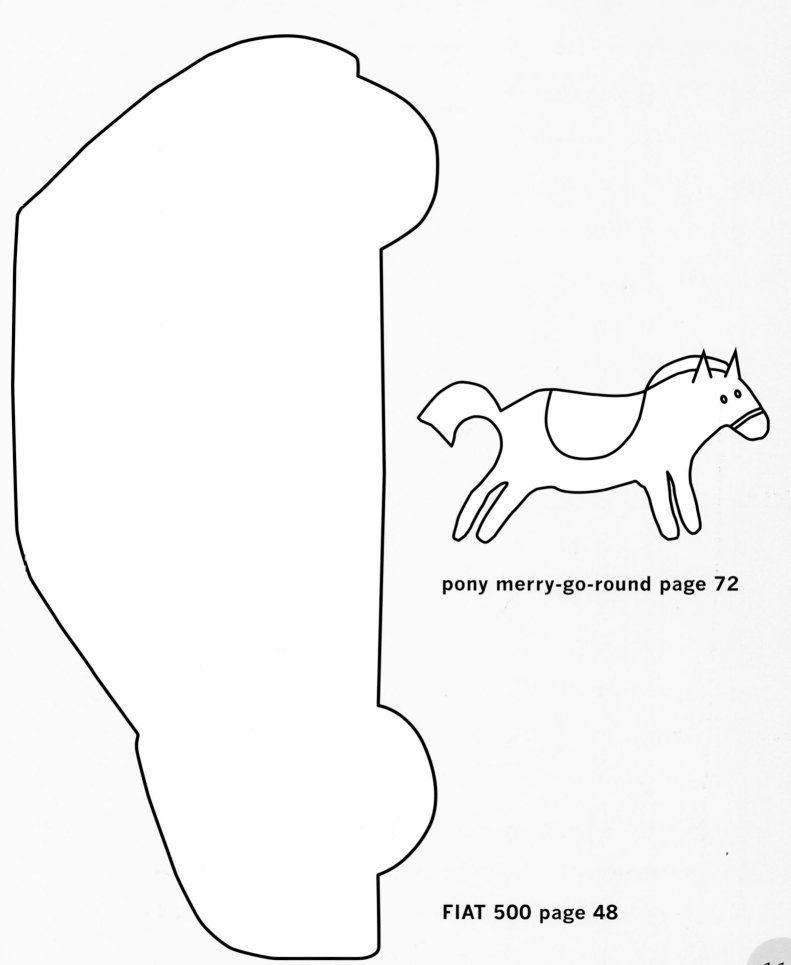

pony merry-go-round page 72

FIAT 500 page 48

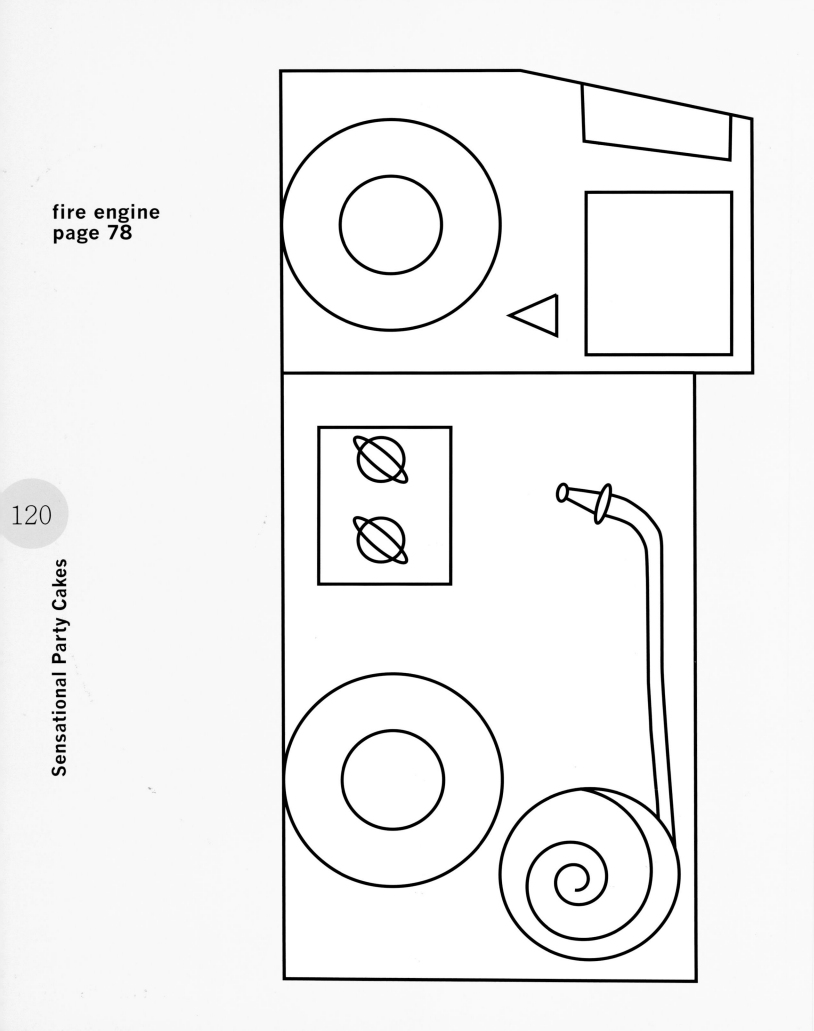

fire engine
page 78

Sensational Party Cakes

panda page 86

Hansel and Gretel's house page 110

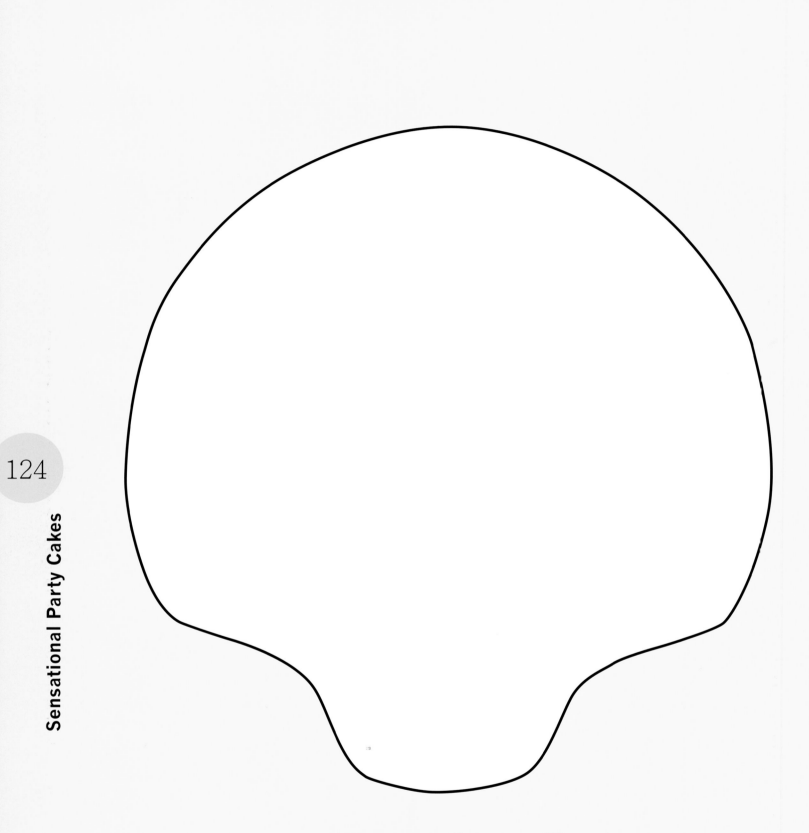

moo-cow cake page 70

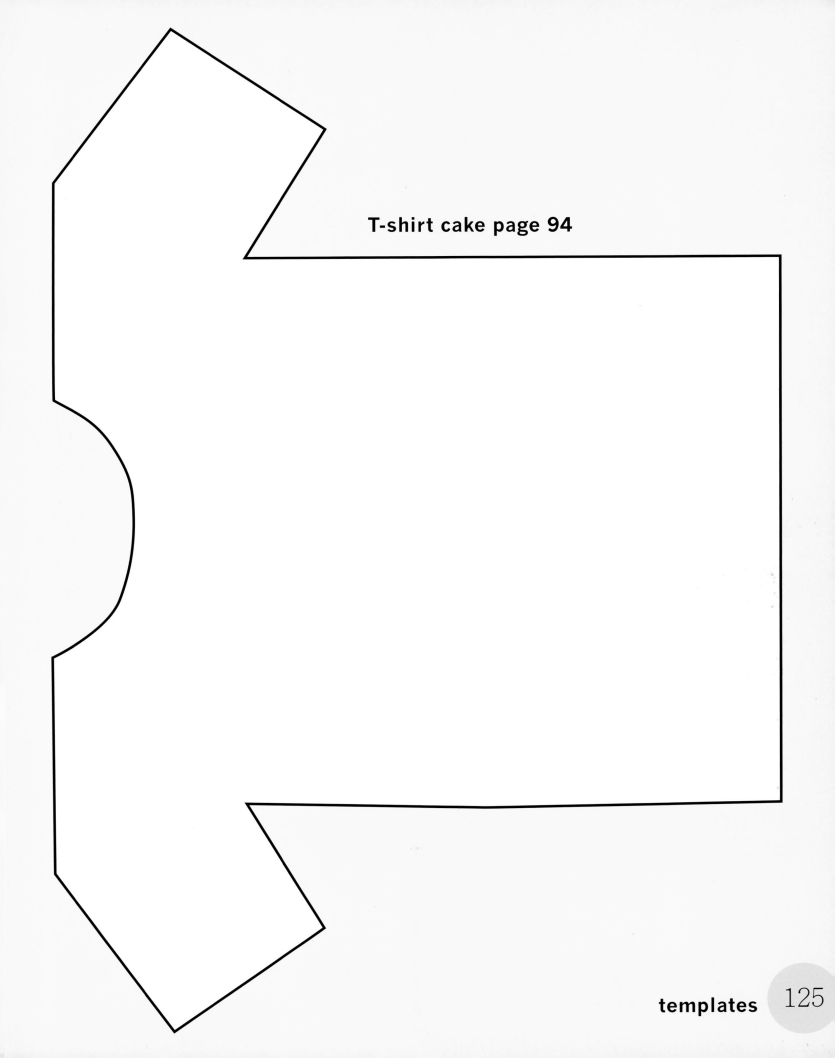

T-shirt cake page 94

index of recipes

Sensational
Party Cakes